THE ORIENTAL INSTITUTE *of* THE UNIVERSITY OF CHICAGO
ORIENTAL INSTITUTE COMMUNICATIONS, NO. 13

TELL ASMAR AND KHAFAJE
THE FIRST SEASON'S WORK IN ESHNUNNA
1930/31

By

HENRI FRANKFORT
THORKILD JACOBSEN
AND
CONRAD PREUSSER

THE UNIVERSITY OF CHICAGO PRESS
CHICAGO, ILLINOIS

ORIENTAL INSTITUTE SERIES

ORIENTAL INSTITUTE COMMUNICATIONS
Illustrated reports describing for the general reader the progress and results of Institute activities

(1) THE ORIENTAL INSTITUTE OF THE UNIVERSITY OF CHICAGO—A BEGINNING AND A PROGRAM. By JAMES HENRY BREASTED. (Out of print.)

(2) EXPLORATIONS IN HITTITE ASIA MINOR—A PRELIMINARY REPORT. By H. H. VON DER OSTEN. (Out of print.)

(3) FIRST REPORT OF THE PREHISTORIC SURVEY EXPEDITION. By K. S. SANDFORD and W. J. ARKELL. 52 pages, royal 8vo, paper $1.00

(4) THE EXCAVATION OF ARMAGEDDON. By CLARENCE S. FISHER. 78 pages, royal 8vo, paper 1.00

(5) MEDINET HABU, 1924–28. By HAROLD H. NELSON and UVO HÖLSCHER. 50 pages, royal 8vo, paper . . . 1.00

(6) EXPLORATIONS IN HITTITE ASIA MINOR, 1927–28. By H. H. VON DER OSTEN. 153 pages, royal 8vo, paper . . 1.00

(7) MEDINET HABU STUDIES, 1928/29. I. THE ARCHITECTURAL SURVEY. By UVO HÖLSCHER. II. THE LANGUAGE OF THE HISTORICAL TEXTS COMMEMORATING RAMSES III. By JOHN A. WILSON. 33 pages, 3 plates, royal 8vo, paper . . . 1.00

(8) EXPLORATIONS IN HITTITE ASIA MINOR, 1929. By H. H. VON DER OSTEN. 196 pages, royal 8vo, paper . . . 2.00

(9) NEW LIGHT FROM ARMAGEDDON. SECOND PROVISIONAL REPORT (1927–29) ON THE EXCAVATIONS AT MEGIDDO IN PALESTINE. By P. L. O. GUY, with a chapter on "An Inscribed Scaraboid" by W. E. STAPLES. 68 pages, royal 8vo, paper . 1.00

(10) MEDINET HABU REPORTS. I. THE EPIGRAPHIC SURVEY, 1928–31. By HAROLD H. NELSON. II. THE ARCHITECTURAL SURVEY, 1929/30. By UVO HÖLSCHER. 69 pages, 4 plates, royal 8vo, paper 1.00

(11) ANATOLIA THROUGH THE AGES. DISCOVERIES AT THE ALISHAR MOUND, 1927–29. By ERICH F. SCHMIDT. 165 pages, royal 8vo, paper 2.00

(12) THE ALPHABET: ITS RISE AND DEVELOPMENT FROM THE SINAI INSCRIPTIONS. By MARTIN SPRENGLING. 71 pages, royal 8vo, paper 1.00

(13) TELL ASMAR AND KHAFAJE. THE FIRST SEASON'S WORK IN ESHNUNNA, 1930/31. By HENRI FRANKFORT, THORKILD JACOBSEN, and CONRAD PREUSSER. 112 pages, royal 8vo, paper 1.50

(14) DISCOVERIES IN ANATOLIA, 1930–31. By H. H. VON DER OSTEN, with the collaboration of R. A. MARTIN and J. A. MORRISON. (In press.) 2.00

(15) EXCAVATIONS AT ANCIENT THEBES, 1930/31. By UVO HÖLSCHER. 65 pages, royal 8vo, paper. (In press.) . . 1.00

THE UNIVERSITY OF CHICAGO PRESS

THE ORIENTAL INSTITUTE
of
THE UNIVERSITY OF CHICAGO

ORIENTAL INSTITUTE COMMUNICATIONS

Edited by
JAMES HENRY BREASTED

with the assistance of
THOMAS GEORGE ALLEN

TELL ASMAR AND KHAFAJE

THE FIRST SEASON'S WORK
IN ESHNUNNA
1930/31

THE UNIVERSITY OF CHICAGO PRESS
CHICAGO, ILLINOIS

THE BAKER & TAYLOR COMPANY
NEW YORK

THE CAMBRIDGE UNIVERSITY PRESS
LONDON

THE MARUZEN-KABUSHIKI-KAISHA
TOKYO, OSAKA, KYOTO, FUKUOKA, SENDAI

THE COMMERCIAL PRESS, LIMITED
SHANGHAI

AIRPLANE VIEW OF TELL ASMAR, WITH DUMP IN FOREGROUND AND WORKMEN'S CAMP IN BACKGROUND

Crown Copyright Reserved

Royal Air Force Official

THE ORIENTAL INSTITUTE of THE UNIVERSITY OF CHICAGO
ORIENTAL INSTITUTE COMMUNICATIONS, NO. 13

TELL ASMAR AND KHAFAJE
THE FIRST SEASON'S WORK IN ESHNUNNA
1930/31

By

HENRI FRANKFORT

THORKILD JACOBSEN

AND

CONRAD PREUSSER

THE UNIVERSITY OF CHICAGO PRESS
CHICAGO, ILLINOIS

THIS BOOK IS NO LONGER THE PROPERTY OF
THE UNIVERSITY OF CHICAGO LIBRARY

COPYRIGHT 1932 BY THE UNIVERSITY OF CHICAGO
ALL RIGHTS RESERVED. PUBLISHED NOVEMBER 1932

COMPOSED AND PRINTED BY THE UNIVERSITY OF CHICAGO PRESS
CHICAGO, ILLINOIS, U.S.A.

OIC No. 13

ERRATA AND ADDENDA

PAGE	LINE	
74	3	*For* 4.50 *read* 4.15.
76	13	*After* meters *insert* (Fig. 31).
76	15	*Delete* as .... (Fig. 31).
80	13	*For* near .... *read* but this can be observed at the east corner only, where the walls show traces of whitewash.
84	4 *from bottom*	*Insert* probably *before* situated.
85	5	*For* 2.50 *read* 2.80.
85	5–6 *from bottom*	*For* run-off .... *read* water which was evidently abundantly used here.
89	11 *from bottom*	*Insert* supposed *before* northeast.
100		*After description of Room XIII insert*

ROOM XIV

This room was separated from the court (Room VIII) by a door the socket stone of which is still *in situ* at the east corner.

110   *Figure 53 should be reversed right for left.*

81939

FOREWORD

The contents of this preliminary report are somewhat unusual in their character. If our account of the excavations at Tell Asmar, at least, appears a little overweighted on the historical side and somewhat slight in purely archeological matter, it must be remembered that it is a first season's work which is discussed here. Starting in a region where no excavations had been previously undertaken, I have deliberately directed our work toward an elucidation of the position which our main site occupied within the framework of Babylonian history during the period to which the ruins we first encountered belonged. I have called, furthermore, upon Dr. Jacobsen's collaboration in no small measure, both in the field and in preparing this report, with a view to utilizing to the full the written documents which we were discovering and which we might hope would give us our bearings in the new area.

Now this report, as a result of its somewhat peculiar character, has not lost weight even though its appearance has been delayed until the third campaign in Eshnunna is about to start. I have, indeed, found no ground for referring here to the discoveries of the second season except in one or two footnotes and in our list of kings, which we wished to bring up to date. For the rest, our original conclusions and inferences are confirmed throughout in a most striking fashion, and the fresh evidence will in turn soon be published.

With the second site which we are excavating in the country of Eshnunna the case is different. The report on Khafaje is purely archeological. But here I have even more consistently refrained from referring to the subsequent work, because Dr. Preusser's departure made it impossible to discuss with him the bearing of the new evidence obtained by his successor, Mr. P. Delougaz, on his own interpretations. I feel the more justified in presenting without any additional notes the valuable results of Dr. Preusser's untiring application to an exceptionally difficult task, since with the appearance of the second preliminary report of this expedition (now in preparation for the press) it will soon become clear on which points a revision of the earlier views is required.

It remains gratefully to acknowledge the support which we have been so fortunate as to receive throughout from all officials of the Iraq Government and of the Mandatory Power with whom we came in contact. We must mention especially here the cordial co-operation of the Department of Antiquities, first under Mr. Sidney Smith, then temporarily under Mr. Lionel Smith, Adviser to the Minister of Education, and finally under Dr. Julius Jordan. Equally valuable was the friendly attitude of the Mutasarrifs of Baghdad, Mosul, and Baquba and their British Advisers. Mr. B. C. Newland, Director of Surveys, assisted us repeatedly with maps and the loan of material. The Air Vice-Marshal commanding, Iraq Command, Royal Air Force, and the officers responsible for air photography, by making an "air mosaic" of Tell Asmar and numerous valuable obliques of both sites in the course of training, have supplied us in our researches with aids the full utility of which is far from being exhausted even now. We hope that the present report may be considered by all of them as justifying to some extent the trouble which they have given themselves in furthering our aims.

HENRI FRANKFORT

LONDON
August 16, 1932

TABLE OF CONTENTS

	PAGE
I. TELL ASMAR, ANCIENT ESHNUNNA. *Henri Frankfort*	1
The Site	1
The Expedition	4
The Excavations	9
II. ESHNUNNA, ELAM, AND AMURRU 2300–1900 B.C. *Henri Frankfort*	25
III. DOCUMENTARY CONTRIBUTIONS TO THE HISTORY AND RELIGION OF ESHNUNNA. *Thorkild Jacobsen*	42
A Seal Inscription of Kirikiri	42
A Building-Inscription of Bilalama	45
"Genealogical" Brick Inscriptions	46
The Successors of Ibiq-Adad II	49
The Chief God of Eshnunna	51
IV. KHAFAJE. *Conrad Preusser*	60
The Site	60
Plano-convex Brickwork	62
The Excavations	63
The Inclosure Walls	65
The Older Structure beneath the Inner Wall	66
The Inner Inclosure Wall	72
The Outer Inclosure Wall	83
The Hooked Wall	86
House D	89
Private Dwellings	105
Graves	107
Conclusion	111

I

TELL ASMAR, ANCIENT ESHNUNNA
By HENRI FRANKFORT

THE SITE

The Diyala, which comes down from the Kurdish mountains and joins the Tigris east of Baghdad (Fig. 1), flows between steep banks and does not fertilize the land. Thus the desert east of the Diyala extends in all directions. But this is not one of nature's deserts; it possesses neither the vastness and pureness of the Libyan sands nor the grandeur of the Egyptian wadies, where the stillness and the dryness inimical to life prevail in a landscape modeled through and through by the torrents of past geological periods. The desert in Iraq shows the desolation of neglect and is the more depressing for being scarred by the ruined works of man. Successions of low ridges are seen everywhere; and when one scrambles across the nearest, one finds a parallel ridge behind it. These are the banks of ancient irrigation canals, raised above plain-level because of the silt thrown up alongside in the annual clearings. Some of the larger hills are strewn with potsherds and bricks; they are all that remains of the ancient towns. For all this gray and dusty country, where now only the winter rains call forth a meager vegetation of small grasses, irises, and anemones which flower with distressing precipitation and wither within a week, was covered with grain fields and teeming cities when there were men to tend the canals and water was abundant.

Tell Asmar (cf. Figs 1 and 4) lies in the midst of this waste, about 50 miles northeast of Baghdad. Once the capital of this region, it is now so indistinguishable from the numerous other town ruins that twice our cars, when we were first reconnoitering these parts, failed to identify it, though in each case some of the party had been there before, and we had to resort to the guidance of wandering Bedawin, whose life depends on their knowledge of the landmarks.

Archeologically this region is *terra incognita*. But during the past two or three years the dealers' shops in Baghdad had suddenly become

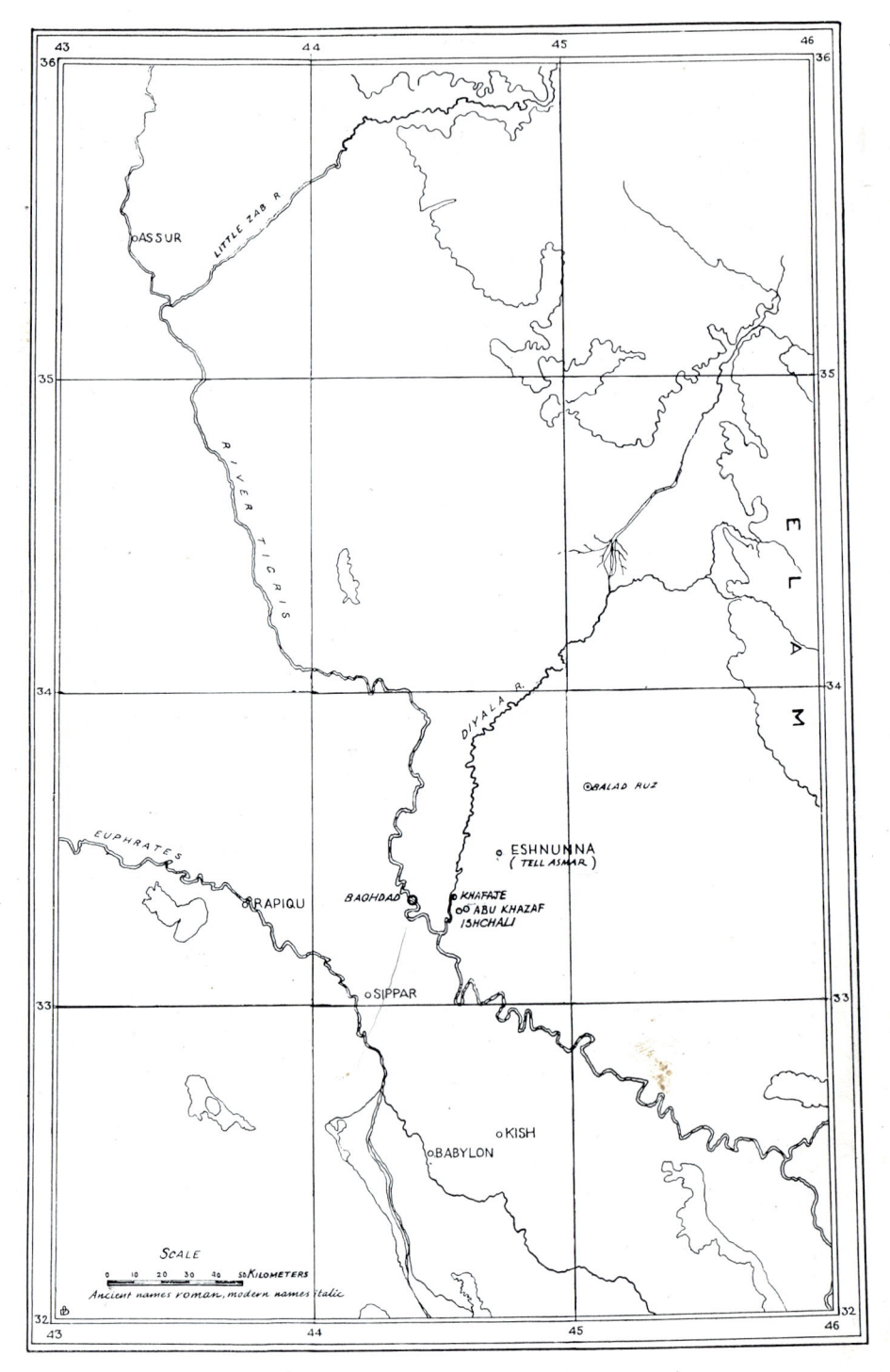

Fig. 1.—Map showing the position of Eshnunna

filled with very valuable objects, mostly dating from early Sumerian times or from the period of Hammurabi's dynasty; and they were said to come from the desert east of the Diyala. Professor Edward Chiera became deeply interested in the idea that the Oriental Institute might undertake excavations there. When the present writer arrived in Baghdad about Christmas of the same year and started to consider the various possibilities which the country offered to the newly organized Iraq Expedition of the Oriental Institute, the director of antiquities, Mr. Sidney Smith, also insisted upon the important results which might be obtained by a systematic exploration of that region and upon the irreparable damage being done by illicit diggers who, by tearing the finds from their archeological context, were destroying their scientific significance. It should be stated here that the expedition's success is in no small degree due to the unstinted support which it received from Mr. Sidney Smith both at this very early stage and later when the work was organized and finally started.

The objects in the dealers' shops had come to a large extent from two mounds in our concession, Khafaje and Ishchali. But some inscribed bricks also had been brought in by the Arabs, and Professor Langdon had been the first to read upon these the name of the ancient city or state of Eshnunna (often called Ashnunnak), which was well known from historical texts but had never been located. Or rather, M. Henri Pognon knew where it was situated and even published in 1892 some brick inscriptions from the site. But he did not divulge the name of the region: "Je m'abstiendrai, dussé-je attendre vingt ans et même mourir sans avoir rien révélé, de faire savoir quelle était la région appelée dans l'antiquité pays d'Achnounnak jusqu'à ce qu'une certaine notabilité scientifique plus influente hélas! que compétente ait disparu ou pris le sage parti de retourner à l'étude de l'archéologie grecque."[1] Unfortunately, M. Pognon disappeared before his friend; and thus in 1929 we were none the wiser for his discovery.

But Professor Chiera had observed that, in the whole of this region east of the Diyala, fragments of inscribed baked bricks were lying about on the surface of only one group of hills. The highest of these

[1] *Le Muséon* XI (1892) 249–53. The quotation is from p. 250 n.

is called by the Bedawin Tell Asmar; here, indeed, he had collected some bricks which mentioned hitherto unknown rulers of Eshnunna. This virgin spot seemed, therefore, the proper place to start our work. For in crossing the Diyala we left known regions behind; though Sumer, and later Babylon and Assyria, had dominated the eastern plain, the latter had retained its individuality and, at least at certain times, more or less independence. At Tell Asmar alone were we certain of finding inscribed bricks on the basis of which we might hope to establish archeological series in a historical framework sufficiently definite to serve later for dating purposes at sites where inscribed bricks might be lacking.

On the other hand, in the East no efficient protection can ever be afforded to ruins by native guards left to themselves. It was imperative to put an end to the illicit digging at Khafaje and Ishchali, twenty miles away from Tell Asmar. Hence it was decided to undertake work at both Khafaje and Tell Asmar. But work at that distance from the expedition's center at Tell Asmar had obviously to be conducted independently. Dr. Conrad Preusser, who had collaborated with Dr. Andrae at Assur before the war and with Dr. Jordan at Warka, was therefore engaged as director of excavations at Khafaje. He was assisted by Mr. Hamilton D. Darby, architect.

THE EXPEDITION

Most of the members of the staff at Tell Asmar were already experienced in excavation in the Near East. Mr. P. Delougaz had been with the Harvard University Expedition at Tarkhalan (Nuzi) and with Professor Chiera at Khorsabad. Messrs. Seton Lloyd and Gordon Loud, architects, had had archeological experience in Egypt, where the former had been engaged with the present writer in the Egypt Exploration Society's work at Tell el-Amarna and the latter had participated in the University of Michigan's excavations in the Faiyum. All of them had been working at Khorsabad the previous winter, as had Dr. Thorkild Jacobsen, fellow of the University of Chicago, who acted as our epigrapher. Mrs. Rigmor Jacobsen was our photographer. Miss G. Rachel Levy, formerly curator of the Palestine Museum, was our recorder.

Though it is the writer's pleasant task to report here on the results of our work, he wishes particularly to draw attention to the pronoun used in this connection. It is, in fact, impossible to distinguish the portion which each of his collaborators or he himself contributed to those results. There certainly has been no detail, either in the practice of the excavations or in the discussion and solving of theoretical problems, which has not been the concern of all; and the enthusiastic and unselfish co-operation in the common cause by all the members of the expedition puts the writer under an obligation toward them which he is anxious to acknowledge here.

Our native labor suffered from a total lack of experience. Through Dr. Preusser we had hired some twenty men from Shergat, and about the same number arrived on their own account. These had worked with the German expedition at Assur; but, though graybeards now, they had been hardly old enough at that time to be trained in that most difficult of the excavator's arts, the clearing of mud-brick walls from soil which differs from them not in material but merely in consistency. At Assur they had been basket-boys, except some six or seven of the oldest; and though that had accustomed them to regular work and, at least by hearsay, to the problems of excavation, they as well as the two hundred locals had to be trained by us. This circumstance delayed the progress of our work considerably, for only detailed supervision and continual checking of what each pick-man was doing could prevent the walls from disappearing at their hands together with the encumbering débris.

Local labor could be called so only with reservations, of course, for the nearest settlement was 15 miles away and some of the men came walking for two or three days when the news spread that money was to be earned at Tell Asmar. These men belonged to the roaming Bedawin whose fierce intertribal fights had ended only with the British occupation during the war. To employ members of different units was a matter of high diplomacy, though not to be dispensed with, for one of the few inducements to prevent *antikas* from being stolen is the fact that one's hereditary enemy is going to make the resulting gain. Our men belonged for the most part to tribal elements which had adopted a semisettled existence, made possible by the work of the Irrigation Department. The latter has already succeeded with the limited means at its disposal in bringing water to places which have been desert since the Middle Ages. Many of the Bedawin have pitched their tents at the tails of the canals, where they grow poor crops of barley and keep chickens, sheep, and a few cows instead of camels. But still the water nearest to Tell Asmar was 12 miles distant. Each batch of workmen, then, before being taken on, entered into negotiations concerning its living conditions. They themselves would send once a week to their villages for flour, eggs, and salt; but we had to lend them material to cover the dugouts which they prepared for themselves (Fig. 2) and, most important of all, to guarantee their water supply. As the water obtainable on the spot appeared only at a depth of over 60 feet and was then so brackish as to be altogether un-

FIG. 2.—Workmen's huts

fit for use, we constructed a series of storage tanks which were filled at regular intervals by journeys of our lorry to the nearest water supply and which held enough water to provide for our settlement of three hundred persons for several days; for the few rainy spells which occur during a Mesopotamian winter turn the desert suddenly into a sea of mud through which no car can pass.

The working-out of these and similar arrangements and the completion of the house somewhat complicated the beginning of the season. The construction of a brick building (Fig. 3) to house the staff and provide workrooms, magazines, etc., had been a formidable undertaking just because of the absence of water. It had been for the most part completed during the summer of 1930 by Abdeljabbar al-Jidda, a Baghdad contractor, while Mr. D. B. Abulafia, a civil engineer from Jerusalem, acted as inspector on our behalf, a task which proved no sinecure. The plans had been prepared during the preceding winter, when the expedition, confined to an adapted native house during a twelve days' spell of rain, had found ample opportunity to meditate on the conditions to which an ideal expedition house should conform! The outcome of these reflections had been put into practicable shape by Messrs. Loud and Lloyd, the main features of the plan being due to the one, while the other was largely responsible for the elevation and for the detailed drawings and specifications on which the contractor depended. Mr. Lloyd came out several weeks earlier than the rest of the staff to supervise and expedite the completion of the house.

FIG. 3.—The expedition house at Tell Asmar

Before describing the actual excavation work, which lasted from November 17, 1930, until March 15, 1931, it may be well to acquaint the reader with our system of recording. An exact survey made by Mr. Loud and showing the state of the ruins before our work started (Fig. 4) serves as a basis. The site is divided into 20-meter squares, indicated by letters and numbers in such a way that the single letters cover the most important part of the site.[1] Within each square, *loci* (none marked in Fig. 4) are distinguished and numbered consecutively. A *locus* may be a room or the corner of a room, a wall, a pot found *in situ*, or in fact any point in any stratum. Thus 1 O 29 is the pit of Urningishzida which we discovered first of all; 7 M 31 is a pavement

[1] In the reproduction of Fig. 4 only 100-meter squares are drawn; but cf. Figs. 6, 7, and 9.

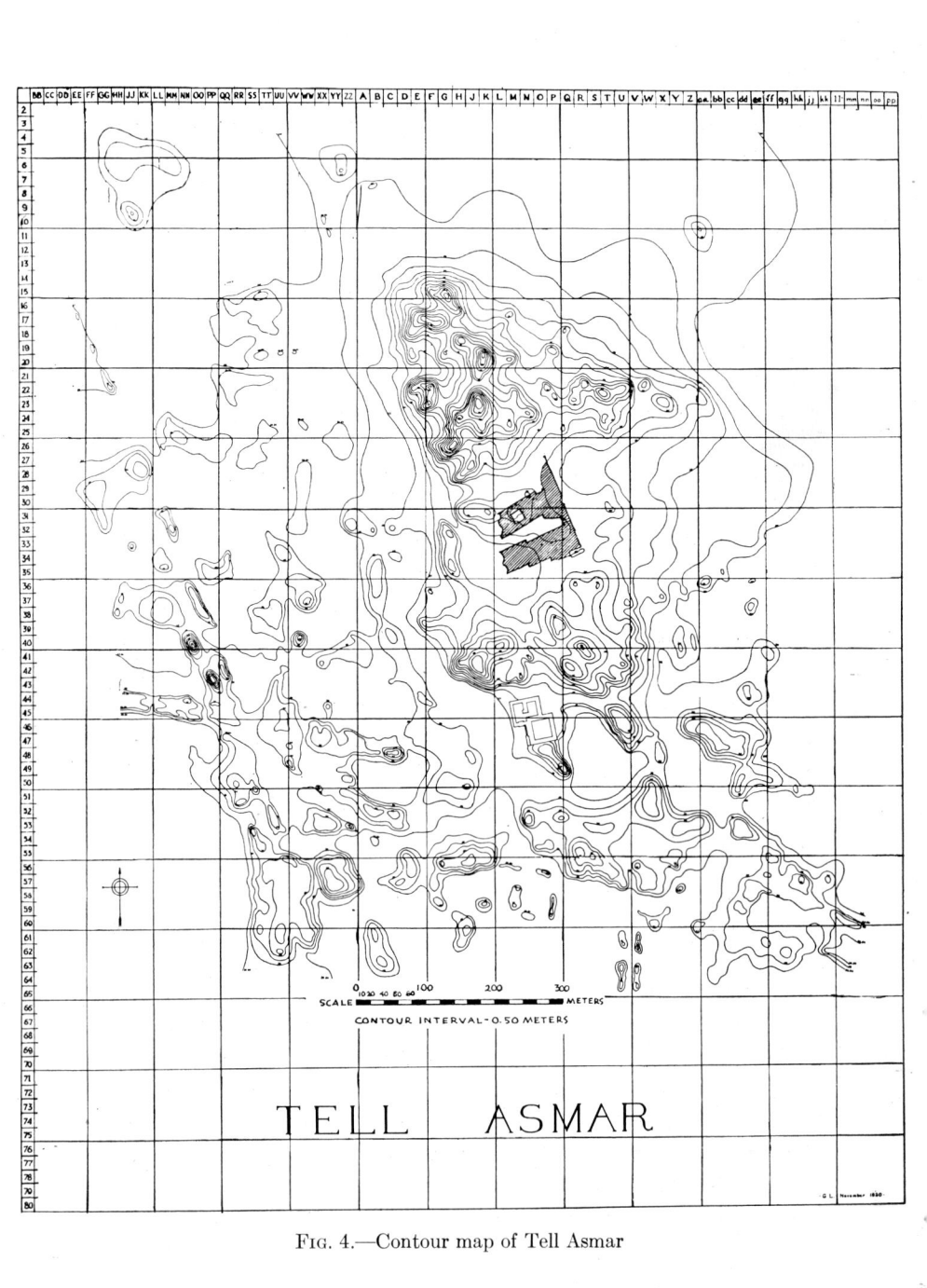

Fig. 4.—Contour map of Tell Asmar

of Ibiq-Adad II of which only a few bricks are left, but which gives important stratigraphical evidence; and so on. This system of reference is simple and has the advantage of allowing each find or observation to be included in the final system of reference from the very first, because the reference does not involve any decision as to the context of the find. This seemed a very considerable advantage over methods of numbering by rooms or by walls or by strata, all of which require decisions as to the circumstances of a find; for it is often impossible to make these at the moment of discovery, when recording should start. The information collected on the *locus* cards, which includes sketches, the depth of the find as recorded by a level, and so on, can then easily be regrouped and studied from all the various points of view and in all the combinations which the development of the work itself suggests.

THE EXCAVATIONS

Since the hope of obtaining historical material from inscribed bricks had brought us to Tell Asmar in preference to other sites in our concession, it was only consistent with our aim that we should begin our excavations on that part of the site where such inscribed bricks were lying about. In one spot we actually found more than mere fragments of inscribed bricks; an excellently made brick pit was visible because the vault had caved in (Fig. 5). The inscriptions on bricks found there ran: "Urningishzida, the beloved of Tishpak, ruler of Eshnunna." There could be no doubt that such a construction belonged to an important building. Our starting-point proved, in fact, to be part of a large complex of buildings where not less than ten rulers of Eshnunna had recorded their building activities by using stamped bricks like the one we first found. If we include date formulas from tablets, our record of local rulers reaches a score.

It would be tedious anticipation of our full and final publication, were we to describe in detail in a report like the present the progress of our work. We may summarize our method by stating that we avoided throughout cutting into the ruins with trenches, but that we tried to develop our excavations organically, following the features of the ruins themselves. Thus, extending our work round the pit in O 29, we soon reached toward the east (Fig. 6) a wall ornamented with recesses and obviously forming at this side the outer inclosure of the building we were investigating. Toward the west we became involved in extensive masses of brickwork in which it was difficult at first to distinguish any particular plan or structure. Carefully feeling our way

FIG. 5.—Tell Asmar before the work started

forward, however, we succeeded in identifying the large square court in M 31 and the groups of rooms which surround it.[1] Henceforward we followed two lines of inquiry. Firstly, from the clear data obtained in the western part of our excavations we worked backward toward

[1] See Oriental Institute *Handbook*, 3d ed. (1931) Fig. 33.

the complicated area between the court and the pit where we had started. And secondly, we used the opportunity offered by the court

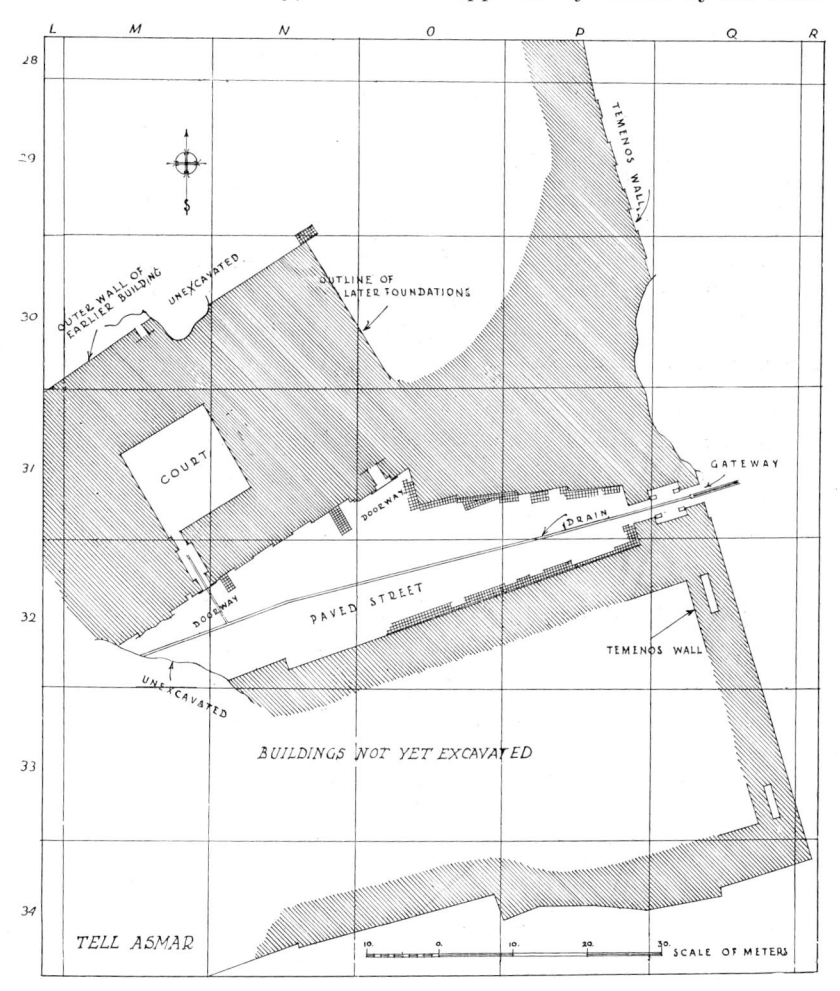

FIG. 7.—Sketch plan of the buildings

to descend into the deeper layers in order to learn from them the history of our site.

Toward the end of the season a third field of inquiry offered itself and was, provisionally at least, explored. The thin grass which appeared after the rains and covered some of the hills of our site did not grow evenly over the surface. Where there were remains of walls just underneath the surface, it scarcely grew at all, whereas it flourished on the looser soil between the walls. Where there was no grass, we could derive information from the color of the soil, which was lighter where the rain water had been absorbed by the loose filling of ancient rooms than it was above ancient walls, where the upper layers remained water-logged and dark. By means of the grass we could follow the walls of a large building which extended immediately south of the one we were excavating. The result is shown in Figure 7, in the lower part of which this new building is seen in outline; two small oblong rooms within its eastern inclosure wall have already been excavated. In Q 31 there is a gateway, where the four boxes of baked brick in which the pivot stones of the doors were imbedded were still in position. A large drain passes outside the building-complex through this gateway. Behind the gateway there is a large paved street or court (Fig. 8), north of which is situated the building with which we were mainly concerned during our first season.

It is obvious that this building and the newly discovered one had been combined into one complex. As far as we know, this was done by the latest ruler of whom we found architectural remains: Ibiq-Adad II, a contemporary of Hammurabi (cf. p. 37). But remains of his time were actually found at the very surface of the soil. Tablets of his reign, written about 1950 B.C., were found cracked by the tiny roots of the desert grass. In only one spot, on the line between N 29 and N 30, a pavement of Ibiq-Adad II (5 N 30) was found intact underneath the loose surface sand; and this was at the very summit of the low hill which covers these ruins. Elsewhere we found only the foundations of his constructions, so strongly have rain, sun, and wind combined to denude the mound. These foundations are shown in outline in Figure 6. West of the N squares none were found; it would seem that Ibiq-Adad II used there the walls of older buildings as foundations. But in the N and O squares his foundations cut down ruthlessly into the older brickwork, which can only with great difficulty be disentangled from the enveloping masses of later bricks. This was the area which for this very reason baffled our understanding at an early stage of the work, as we have mentioned above. Part of it was completely filled to form a solid brick platform upon which

FIG. 8.—The street between the two buildings, looking east

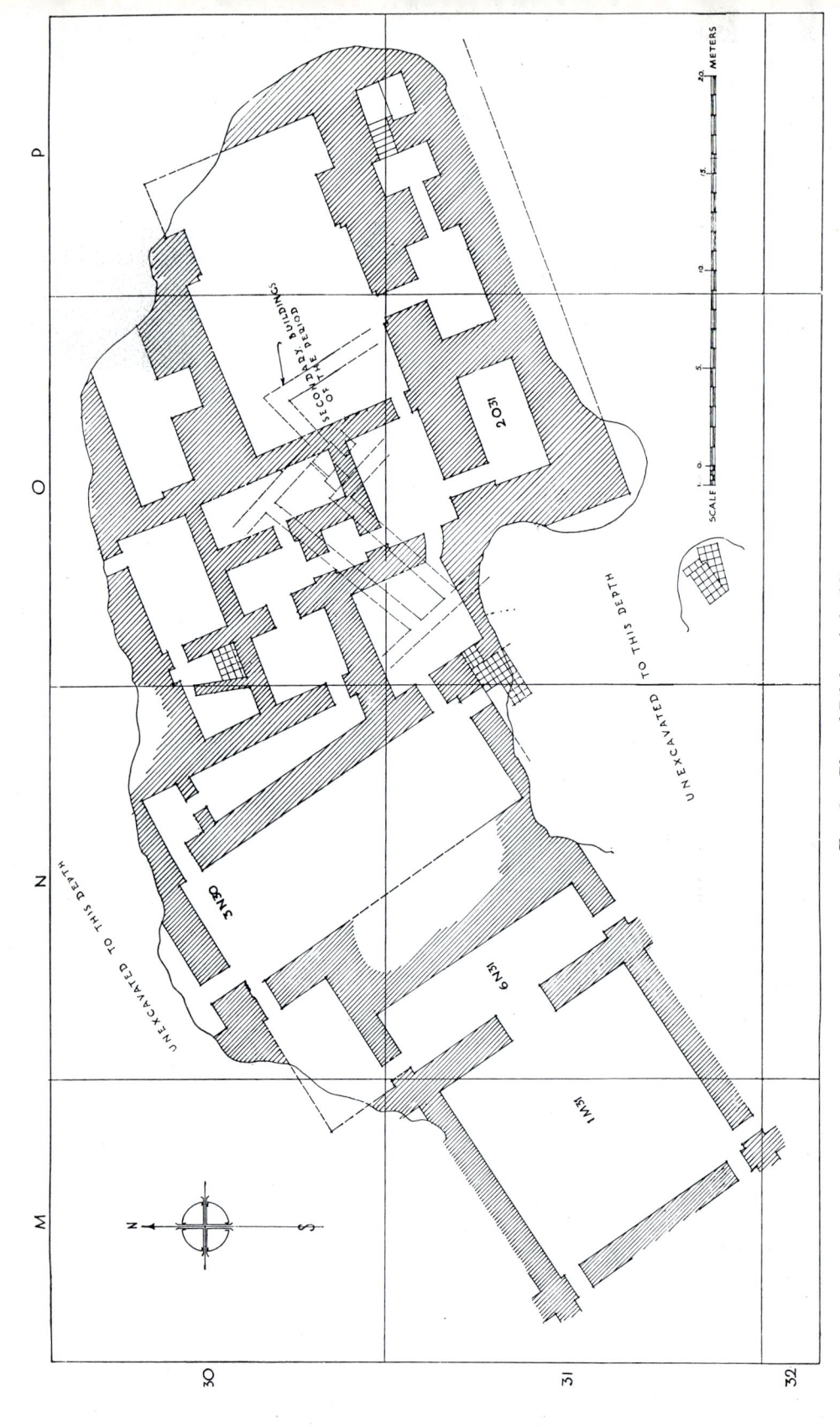

FIG. 9.—Plan of Bilalama's building

Ibiq-Adad II's building rested. The deeper layers reveal why such far-reaching innovations were carried out in just this part of the building. At this point two originally separate buildings, differently oriented, had been joined together. This is particularly clear in the plan of the old building of Bilalama (Fig. 9). Ibiq-Adad may have found for this part of the building a less unsightly solution which made the utilization of the old walls impracticable.

A further complication made it well-nigh impossible to gain a clear insight into the constructions of the various periods at this point.

FIG. 11.—Ibalpel's pit

Figure 10 shows that the Bilalama level (II) extends almost horizontally through the site, but that from Urninmar onward the levels slope upward toward the east. This in turn seems due to a wish on the part of the builder, in this case Urninmar, to get rid of a number of older constructions by covering them. It will be seen in Figure 9 that after the destruction of Bilalama's palace various secondary buildings of a flimsy character were built on the eastern part of the site. These were covered by Urninmar's leveling, with the result that the floor levels of Urninmar and of all the rulers who succeeded him are higher in the eastern part of the ruins than round the court 1 M 31.

On the other hand, since the surface of the hill slopes downward toward the east, we have irretrievably lost on that side the layers corresponding with the perfectly well preserved upper strata round the court. For instance, we found in P 30 a round pit (Fig. 11) of baked bricks bearing the imprint of Ibalpel, the father of Ibiq-Adad II. Its vault is worth special attention: the bricks were laid in two semicircles, each propped up on fragments in the middle, so that the superimposed courses would gradually converge and eventually meet. The bricks used in building this pit are ordinary square ones, though segmented bricks specially made to serve in circular buildings were found in secondary use in several places on the site. The spaces at the outside of the circle, due to the use of square bricks, were neatly filled with fragments. Now a little street paved with bricks led down from Ibalpel's building to the pit, but it disappeared suddenly at the surface of the soil: the ground had been denuded below even this pavement level. Yet the western part of the building (see Fig. 6) was used and restored by Ibalpel; he heightened the walls and provided them with a facing of baked bricks (cf. Figs. 10 and 15). Of this facing only the lowest courses remain, as becomes clear if we consider that the great drain of baked bricks which carried off the rain water from the large court through its southwestern gateway was here found almost at the surface of the hill, emerging above the remains of Ibalpel's facing, whereas originally it must have run below the pavement of the court.

A bitumen-covered doorsill belonging to Ibalpel's edifice was found in O 31. Below this we discovered a similar entrance, but with four steps (Fig. 12), belonging to the level of Ibiq-Adad I, Ibalpel's grandfather. Farther west, in M 32, we assume that there was another entrance; for there a large mass of baked brickwork of Ibiq-Adad I rested upon a similar solid construction of his father Urninmar, and drains made of bricks stamped by these and later kings left the building at this point.[1] Though we are still at a loss to explain why an entrance should be built with such a costly foundation, there seems no doubt as to the meaning of this part of the building. Outside we found remains of two drains built of bricks bearing inscriptions considerably longer than those we had found so far; they were of great importance, as they named Naramsin as son of Ibiq-Adad, and Ibalpel

[1] See *ibid*. Fig. 31.

FIG. 12.—Entrance to Ibalpel's building, partly broken away so that the entrance stairs of Ibiq-Adad I appear farther down.

as son of Dadusha (see pp. 35–36). The conclusion which we had already reached on the basis of our stratification, that there must have been two kings named Ibiq-Adad, was thus confirmed.

The southern front of the building was decorated with recesses such as we had previously noticed at the eastern limit of our excavations (cf. p. 9); at two points, moreover, there was a sloping pavement of baked bricks to prevent the rain water from penetrating into the foundations of the wall.

It is obvious that very little can be said at the present stage of our work about the nature and purpose of this building. We have called

Fig. 13.—Tunneling into the ruins. General view of excavated structures, looking west.

it a "palace" because we need a designation, and also because it is clear that a building reconstructed so often by the rulers of the city can have been only a palace or a temple. That it was a temple is highly improbable. There is no room off the main court which could be considered to be the cella. Moreover, we know the name of the main temple of Eshnunna and have found bricks belonging to it (see p. 25), and they bear a different imprint from those used in this building. There remains the possibility that this was not the temple itself but some building closely connected with it, such as the temple stores. This possibility cannot be ruled out, but the whole question can obviously not be solved until our work is very much more advanced.

Underneath the layer of Urninmar were several poor constructions built on the burned ruins of an earlier palace (Fig. 9). This was built by Bilalama, or rather restored and enlarged by him. A huge conflagration has preserved the walls so well that we are certain of obtaining a very complete plan of the whole of this building as soon as the superimposed remains have been sufficiently investigated and can be removed. Till now we have had to trace its walls to a large extent by means of tunnels (Fig. 13). A fine court in the eastern part of the building seems to have had a wide niche between two ornamental piers at its eastern end (Fig. 9).

Bilalama was not the original builder of the palace. He heightened the floors and walls of an existing building the baked bricks of

FIG. 14.—Lapis lazuli cylinder seal given by Kirikiri to his son Bilalama

which are not inscribed. But we assign it to Bilalama's father, whose name, Kirikiri, has been preserved on a magnificent lapis lazuli cylinder seal (Fig. 14; cf. p. 42). The succession of remains may be seen very clearly in Figure 15, which shows the northwest corner of the large court 1 M 31. The baked bricks at the right-hand top of the figure are the lowest layers of the baked-brick facing with which the walls were provided by Ibalpel. In the section (Fig. 10) it can be seen that above this, projecting into the court, were a few bricks remaining from a pavement of Ibiq-Adad II. There one may observe also how the strata in the various parts of the excavation correspond. For instance, the successive building-periods which can be observed in the mass of baked brick on the west side of the court are equally well marked in the various frontages on which the eastern wall of the court (in the section between 1 M 31 and 6 N 31) was rebuilt.

FIG. 15.—Northwest corner of Court 1 M 31, showing successive floor levels

To return to our Figure 15, we notice below the revetment of Ibalpel a nameless mud brick wall; its builder may have been Dadusha, Ibalpel's father. That it is an independent level is shown by the properly finished doorsill and rebates just visible in the middle of our picture. A little lower, but showing at the same height in the picture, we see some baked bricks from a drain of Ibiq-Adad I. This drain was originally situated underneath the pavement of the court, the western wall of which down to this level is not visible in the photograph. The reason is that Ibiq-Adad I enlarged the court considerably, so that the western wall of his day stands well back and cannot be seen from the low level at which the photograph was taken. From here downward, however, we see the actual corner of the court. The highest baked-brick pavement of which the edge is visible in both walls dates from Urninmar, but contains also bricks of two other rulers (cf. p. 33). Below that is a pavement put down by Bilalama; on the plaster of the wall at the right appear traces of the conflagration. The edge of the doorway leading toward the west can also be distinguished, though this feature is clearer in the earlier building, of which the baked-brick facing and the edge of the pavement of the court show very clearly. This earlier building is that of the anonymous ruler whom we suppose to be Kirikiri, Bilalama's father.[1] As our men penetrated into yet deeper layers, it was found that entirely different structures had previously existed at this spot. Figure 10 shows the location of a kiln where pottery was baked. Farther toward the west, but also in the court in O–P 30, tablets with year dates of the 3d dynasty of Ur were found.

A few words will suffice to account for the objects found in our palace. Terra cotta figurines, tablets, and copper or bronze weapons are the most important. The first mentioned group contains two main types: one, a naked female figure with elaborately dressed hair; the other, a bearded figure, wearing sometimes a "Hittite" pointed cap, sometimes the divine crown with horns, and holding some animal in his hands (Figs. 16–17). Some of the male figures may well represent Tishpak, the chief god of Eshnunna, about whom Dr. Jacobsen makes some interesting remarks on pages 51–59.[2] A unique object (Fig. 18)

[1] Cf. p. 27, n. 1.
[2] It may not be too bold to see in the object which some of these figures hold before them a crude rendering of the missile referred to in the myth of Labbu, namely, the "seal of the throat" (see pp. 53–54).

22   TELL ASMAR, ANCIENT ESHNUNNA

showing the heads of a bull, an ibex, and a lion, which could be rotated round a pin stuck through a hole in the center, we should like to think of as used in astrological divination; at least the nature of the animals

FIG. 16.—Typical terra cotta figurines representing men carrying animals. Scale, 4:5.

seems to suggest this. But we publish it in this preliminary report largely to give scholars better versed in this subject an opportunity to support or refute our guess.

The Excavations 23

Fig. 17.—Terra cotta figurines perhaps representing Tishpak. Scale, about 3:4

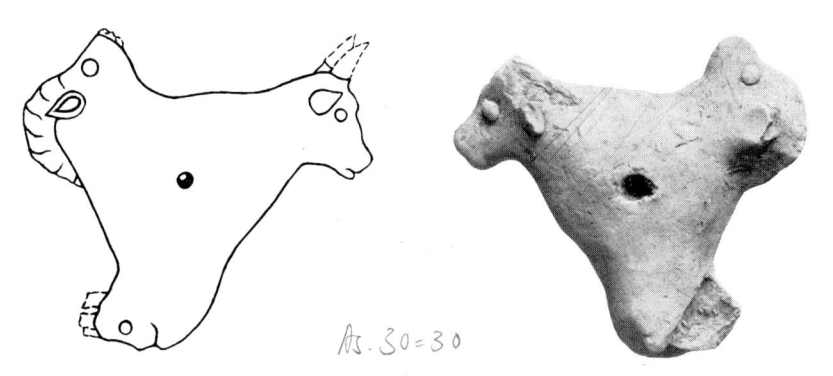

Fig. 18.—Terra cotta object perhaps of astrological significance

The tablets, which number about six hundred, contain, besides the contracts and other business documents which one would expect, a few letters to the rulers of Eshnunna which are of particular interest. The main importance of the tablets at the moment is found in their date formulas; these, in conjunction with the brick inscriptions and the stratigraphical observations made in the palace, enable us to outline in some detail the history of Eshnunna during the period with which we are concerned.

II

ESHNUNNA, ELAM, AND AMURRU
2300–1900 B.C.
By HENRI FRANKFORT

It will have become clear from the foregoing account that the remains unearthed in our first season's work at Tell Asmar do not cover a long period of time; in fact, they represent altogether less than four centuries. But it so happens that during this period Eshnunna played an important part in the history of Babylonia, and thus our material bears on problems of more than merely local significance. The period includes the troubled centuries after the fall of the 3d dynasty of Ur; and our finds reveal that Eshnunna stood in close contact with both the main elements in the subsequent situation: the Elamites and the Amorites. Finally, Eshnunna was one of the active opponents of Hammurabi when he attempted to restore order and welfare by a unification of the valley of the Two Rivers. It seems indicated, then, that we should include in this report an attempt to place our discoveries within this wider context and to see in what way they elucidate the course of events during those fateful years.

The first result of our work has been to remove any doubt as to the identification of Tell Asmar with ancient Eshnunna. The palace would scarcely have been restored and rebuilt by so many *ishakkus* of Eshnunna, sometimes, as in the case of Urninmar, even twice in one reign, if it had not been of vital importance to these rulers. We have, moreover, corroborative evidence in the form of several baked bricks of Bilalama found on the site, some of them built into our palace, which refer to another building still to be discovered, namely, E-sikil, which they state that Bilalama built for the god Tishpak (cf. p. 45). From the list of Sumerian sanctuaries published by Zimmern[1] we know that E-sikil was situated in the city of Eshnunna.

As usual in Babylonia, the domain of the *ishakku* included a certain amount of the country around his city, which was likely under a

---

[1] *Zeitschrift für Assyriologie* XXXIX (1930) 267.

successful ruler to develop into the capital of a small state. Hence it is not always possible to decide whether texts recording conquests refer to the town or to the state. The extent of this state of Eshnunna under several rulers we can already estimate to a certain degree. A baked brick inscribed by Urningishzida was found on the Balad Ruz estate, about 50 miles northeast of Tell Asmar (see Fig. 1); to the west and southwest we may include all the land up to the Diyala. That even Baghdad, between the Diyala and the Tigris, lies in Eshnunna territory is indicated by the date formulas on various tablets found by illicit diggers at Ishchali, at Khafaje, and near Alwiya on the outskirts of Baghdad. These tablets, which have been examined by Dr. Jacobsen, will, in so far as they have been bought for the Institute's collections, be published in course of time. They follow the local system of dating by events in the reigns of the *ishakkus* of Eshnunna: Naramsin, Dadusha, Ibalpel, and Belakum. The first-named of these actually ruled Sippar; for there can be little doubt that he is referred to in the date formula of a tablet from that city which, as Ungnad has shown,[1] belongs probably to the period of Sumuabu in which our ruler also is approximately to be placed. We shall see, furthermore, that the historical conditions at the time favor the identification.

The history of Eshnunna during this period can already be outlined with the help of the material recovered in our first season. One fact stands out with unmistakable clearness: the fate of Eshnunna, for better or for worse, was closely bound up with that of Elam, the mountainous country east of the Tigris. It was an inroad of the Elamites which put an end to the 3d dynasty of Ur, the seat of power during the last and most glorious development of Sumerian culture. We have not yet evidence of the existence of a palace in this period. We know of rulers of Eshnunna at that time who were but governors under the kings of Ur; and some documents dated in the reigns of Shulgi and Gimilsin were found in the oldest layers reached by our excavations. But beneath the square open court in the center of the later palace there had been only pottery kilns in the time of the 3d dynasty of Ur (cf. Fig. 10). The palace may have been founded after the fall of that dynasty. Its baked bricks are uninscribed; but as it was reconstructed by Bilalama and as we have a beautiful cylinder seal

[1] *Orientalistische Literaturzeitung* XII (1909) 478–79.

given to Bilalama by his father Kirikiri (see Fig. 14 and p. 42), who was likewise *ishakku* of Eshnunna, there is good reason to suppose that Kirikiri was the builder of the palace and founder of the dynasty of independent kings.[1] His name is significant, for it is certainly neither Sumerian nor Akkadian, but, whatever its precise affinities may be, belongs most probably to that little known group of languages spoken by the peoples of the eastern mountains. We may well argue, therefore, that the rise of Eshnunna as an independent power was due to its ruler's relations with the conquerors who defeated the 3d dynasty of Ur. Most likely Kirikiri entered the country together with the Elamites and received Eshnunna as his share of the spoil. In any case Dr. Jacobsen's analysis of the eighty personal names which occur on our tablets of this period has not revealed among the population a corresponding foreign strain; in fact, three-quarters of the names are purely Akkadian.

In thus reconstructing the origin of the independent dynasty of Eshnunna it may seem as though we have been building a heavy structure on a flimsy foundation. But we have much more than the name of Kirikiri to go by. His son Bilalama maintained intimate relations with Elam; for Danrukhuratir, king of Susa, married Bilalama's daughter Mekubi, as a text found at Susa shows.[2] Finally, there is a significant parallelism in the histories of Eshnunna and Elam in this period. For the reigns of both Bilalama and Danrukhuratir were followed by a dark period which was not one of quiet development. The palace of Bilalama was destroyed by a huge conflagration, traces of

[1] We now know, after our second season at Tell Asmar, that the palace was founded in the reign of Ibisin (see king list, pp. 40–41); but it remains true that Kirikiri was the founder of a new and independent dynasty.

[2] "Mémoires de la Délégation en Perse" II (1900) 80; *ibid.* XIV (1913) 24 f.; and Thureau-Dangin, *Die sumerischen und akkadischen Königsinschriften* (Leipzig, 1907) p. 180, No. 3. Dr. Jacobsen adds to this: "According to this inscription Mekubi, the wife of Danrukhuratir, was the daughter of one Bil-la-ma (var., Bí-la-ma, 'Mémoires . . . .' XIV 24), *ishakku* of Eshnunna. The identity of this Bil-la-ma with the *ishakku* Bilalama who occurs in the texts from Eshnunna is obvious. That the name, which in Eshnunna is always written Bí-la-la-ma, occurs as Bil-la-ma and Bí-la-ma in Susa would seem to indicate that the first *a* of the name was pronounced so indistinctly that it could escape altogether the ear of a foreigner. That the Elamite scribe omitted by mistake one of the two *la*-signs in Bilalama's name is not likely; for the inscription has come down to us in two handwritten copies, both of which write the name with only one *la*."

which are evident all over the palace area and to the full present height of the walls, of which in some places 2 or 3 meters are still standing. This excludes the possibility of an accidental fire, which would have been easy to master in a building consisting largely of thick walls of unbaked bricks. Obviously Eshnunna was taken and its main buildings destroyed.

Before we proceed to investigate the cause of this catastrophe, we must consider a few more date formulas which are of exceptional importance. The material adduced above concerned Bilalama's connections with Elam; these formulas elucidate in a most unusual manner his relations with the other dominant power of the period, the Amorites; Semitic nomads from the North Syrian desert and the region west of the middle Euphrates.[1] They had been employed occasionally in various tasks and in small numbers in the time of the 3d dynasty of Ur. Now they swarmed all over the country in more or less numerous bands. Gimilsin had been obliged to build a "wall of Amurru" to keep his northwestern neighbors in check. His successor, Ibisin,

[1] See for the latest full discussion on "Amorites" Sidney Smith, *Early History of Assyria* (London, 1928) pp. 176 ff. and 371, n. 17. We quote from his p. 177: "This term must not be interpreted strictly as referring to a group that form a linguistic or even a racial unity. For the Babylonian, Amurru was a purely geographical term, used rather vaguely." Bauer has tried to give to this term a linguistic connotation which it does not possess; and he has, when the discrepancy became clear, attempted to remodel history on philological material alone.

Dr. Jacobsen points out to me that an inscription of Lugalannimundu, of the 1st dynasty of Adab, mentions MAR.TU in connection with the Sutu, another indication that the lands on the middle Euphrates were populated in a very early period by the "Amorites" of Babylonian terminology. He adds:

"Perhaps the strongest of the arguments which Landsberger and Bauer have put forward in support of their thesis that the KUR.MAR.TU people are quite different from the 'East Canaaneans' is the fact that no true 'East Canaanean' names occur among the names of those people who in texts from the 3d dynasty of Ur are definitely designated by the term 'MAR.TU.'

"But is this really the case? In Pater Schneider's recent work on the Drehem and Jokha texts he quotes three MAR.TU names which, as far as I can see, have a definitely 'East Canaanean' appearance. The names are *ià-an-pil-li-nim*, *ià-an-pu-li*, and *ià-a-mu-tum* (*Orientalia* No. 23 [1927] Nos. 2414, 2415, 2407; the third name is corrected with the text as published by Genouillac, *Tablettes de Dréhem* [Paris, 1911] No. 5508 i 12). The first of these could quite well contain a hiphil of a root *n p l* and might tentatively be explained as *ianpil-li-na* (Akkadianized to

the last king of Ur, reports once how he brought into submission "the Amurru, a host (whose onslaught was) like a hurricane, (a people) who had never known a city," terms which express, as Mr. Gadd rightly remarks, "the highly-civilized townsman's wondering disgust at the incredible barbarity of the nomads."[1] In the following centuries we find that at various times in Kish and Isin, in Babylon, and even in

---

i̯anpillinum, gen. i̯anpillinim), 'He (the god) has made (the lot) fall for us (i.e., in our favor),' meaning 'We have had luck,' namely, in getting a boy. Cf. Arabic نفل and Hebrew נפל 'to fall,' of lots. Similarly i̯anpuli may be a qal form, i̯anpul-li, 'It (the lot) falls for me.' For the last name I venture no explanation.

"These names put the material from Drehem and Jokha in a new light. Of about 30 names the bearers of which are designated by the term 'MAR.TU,' 11 end in -ānum, 9 are plain Sumerian or Akkadian, while 3, as shown above, look very much like 'East Canaanean.'

"In a case like this the Sumero-Akkadian names are of no help in determining the nationality of the bearer, because very often foreigners will adopt names from the country in which they live. The names in -ānum are claimed by Bauer and Landsberger to represent an Akkadian dialect, but in the discussion following the appearance of Bauer's book it was rightly stressed by Lewy that this ending is frequent in Syrian names of the Amarna period and occurs in geographical names from this region (e g., armanum, labnanum) as early as the dynasty of Agade. It is, therefore, in all probability West Semitic.

"It appears, then, that of the MAR.TU people in the Drehem texts 3 have names which look exactly like the so-called 'East Canaanean' names; 11, the -ānum names, have strong affinities with West Semitic nomenclature; and the 9 which are Sumero-Akkadian may well have been assumed by the MAR.TU people in their new surroundings. It seems to me, therefore, that this material points rather to the *identity* of these people with the West Semitic 'East Canaaneans' than to the opposite."

[1] Gadd, *History and Monuments of Ur* (London, 1929) p. 126. I am unable to resist the temptation of quoting here a delightful passage from a text published and translated by Professor Chiera (Crozer Theological Seminary, "Babylonian Publications" I [1924] 20–21) which describes the contrast between the states of the Amorite before and after he had settled in Babylonia:
"For the mountaineer (i.e., the Amorite)
  the weapon (is his) companion . . . . ,
  he digs the *kamunu* by the side of the mountain, he knows no submission,
  he eats uncooked meat,
  through his whole life he does not possess a house,
  his dead companion he does not bury.
(Now) Martu possesses a house(?);
  towards his house Adgaruddug turns.
(Now) Martu possesses grain.
O Ninab, grow luxuriantly."

Kazallu east of the Tigris, on the southern borders of Eshnunna, the power was in the hands of these foreigners. As Mr. Smith remarks: "The invasion of Babylonia by these foreigners was, then, not a concerted invasion by a people led by a single conqueror; it was rather a case in which the foreign element introduced by peaceful means spasmodically seized the rule in certain cities and fought indifferently with the settled inhabitants or one another, according to their temporary interest."[1]

In fact, our suggestion above, that the 3d dynasty of Ur fell before an inroad of the Elamites, has presented a rather simplified version of what happened. Ibisin of Ur was captured by Ishbiirra, a man from Mari on the middle Euphrates, whom we are fully entitled, therefore, to call an Amorite.[2] He had obtained for himself a foothold in Isin and from there, allied with Elam, the great power in the East, attacked Ur. That Elam held the sovereign position is proved beyond doubt by the fact that Ishbiirra had to send his chief captive, the ruler of Ur, to Susa. That, on the other hand, Elam employed the Amorite instead of acting itself can be explained by the consideration, recently stressed again by F. W. König, that the center of gravity of Elam lay well toward the east, in the mountains, a fact which we are liable to neglect because for us the importance of Elam lies entirely in the part it plays in Babylonian history. Yet all the activities which for us constitute the main part of Elamite history take place on the periphery of that country. This circumstance also explains an anomaly which we note a few generations later and which has given rise to a number of ingenious speculations. An Elamite, Kudurmabug, was then the most powerful figure in Babylonia. It is likely that he was the head of the royal family of Elam; but he was not the ruler of Elam, for the latter (not unlike the negus of Abyssinia) was a king of kings and resided in the east. Kudurmabug was only one of these Elamite kings, subject to the king of kings, if we consider him within the framework of the whole of Elam. But as he ruled an outlying portion of Elamite territory in the plain east of the Tigris (called Yamutbal), he could act with complete independence in all matters which

[1] Smith, *op. cit.* p. 178.

[2] *Ibid.* p. 176. It is quite characteristic for the situation at the time that Ibisin of Ur should engage Amorites on his side also to fight Ishbiirra.

interest us and which we view not from the Elamite but from the Babylonian standpoint.[1]

This digression has been necessary, not only to present an alternative to certain recent views regarding the country of origin of the Amorites, but also to explain the position of Ishbiirra. And this again provides the requisite basis for judging the exceptional value of the four date formulas of Bilalama which we are about to discuss. For they show that exactly the same relation which existed between the Elamites and the Amorites existed also between the Amorites and Eshnunna, and they reveal by their explicitness the working of this conspiracy against the existing order. Bilalama's date formulas read as follows:

"Year when Amurru destroyed Ka-ibaum" (Tell Asmar 248)
"Year when Badbar and Ka-ibaum were built" (T.A. 252)
"Year when Amurru destroyed Ishur" (T.A. 246)
"Year when Amurru intrusted Bilalama with the rule of Ishur" (T.A. 253)

The last formula, in its completeness, contains the key to the understanding of all of them. It appears that the Amorites ravaged and plundered cities in the neighborhood with the connivance of Bilalama, who annexed and rebuilt them after the nomads had taken the loot which constituted their exclusive interest in those towns. By analogy with the last two formulas the first two can hardly be interpreted in

[1] The original suggestion of Weidner (*Die Könige von Assyrien* [in "Mitteilungen der Vorderasiatisch-Aegyptischen Gesellschaft" XXVI (1921)] 43), who would designate as Amurru all the country east of the Tigris from the border of Yamutbal up to Assur, could be used to explain Kudurmabug's title. We shall see (our p. 36) that this was exactly the country which was dominated by Rimsin; and it is possible that the Elamites named all that part of their territory which was not inhabited by "Japhethite" mountaineers but by Semites (namely, Akkadians and recently arrived groups of Amorites, more prominent because more troublesome) after one of those Semitic tribes. The argument was vitiated only when it was attempted to put this nomenclature on a purely philological basis. Even so, Weidner may read into the title "father" or "patron" of Amurru more than it contains. *Adda* may have been a title borne by the venerable head of the royal family of Elam, if with König (*Geschichte Elams* ["Der Alte Orient" XXIX (1931)] 28) we explain Kudurmabug's position in this way. Moreover, the title is most suitable to express that peculiar and purely personal authority which a man of Kudurmabug's power and ability might exercise over a large, incoherent, and unorganized mass of Bedawin. It is more than likely that this authority had grown on the basis of the relation which had existed since the days of Ishbiirra. Schnabel (*Göttingische Gelehrte Anzeigen* CLXXXIX [1927] 51) maintains that the title was assumed after the conquest of Amorite Larsa.

any other way, especially when we remember that these date formulas name events of local importance, so that the "building" (which we understand to be "rebuilding") of Badbar and Ka-ibaum must have been done by Bilalama. It seems justifiable to assume that Bilalama came to this working agreement with the formidable "Westerners" as a means of keeping them away from his own territory; in fact, another date formula runs: "Year when Amurru made submission" (T.A. 262). This shows that relations between the partners had not always been peaceful; and the term "submission" may well hide the actual understanding according to which the Amorites left Eshnunna alone, on condition that certain other cities were to be their prey. It would, of course, be useless for Bilalama merely to mention these cities to the Amorites; we may assume that he had to support the latter by a contingent of troops, to make sure that the skin of the bear, having been sold, was also delivered.

It would be of great interest if we could locate these cities, but at present we cannot. The fact that they were incorporated in Eshnunna, a state the center of which lay east of the Tigris, does not help us at all; for we have seen at the beginning of this chapter that various later rulers extended their territory far toward the west, and Bilalama appears to us no less powerful. As we find him in our records, allied by marriage with the king of Susa, using the roaming Amorites for his own purposes, building palaces and temples in his capital, he is the most splendid figure yet distinguishable among the rulers of Eshnunna. Yet his rule, or that of his successor, ended in a disaster to which the ruins of his palace bear witness.[1]

Times of catastrophe leave records too confused for us satisfactorily to disentangle the course of events. In the ruins of the palace we find records of three more rulers. Of these, Isharramashu may perhaps be Bilalama's immediate successor; or he may have ruled still later, arranging his quarters in the ruins as best he could. This certainly was done by Aṣuṣu, whom we may therefore date definitely after the catastrophe. But the remaining ruler, Uṣurawasu, may well be connected with the catastrophe itself. Jar-sealings style him "*ishakku* of Eshnunna" with the usual epithets. But on one tablet (T.A. 245) we find "Uṣurawasu, the man of Der," and on another (T.A. 222)

[1] We now know that the conflagration took place under Bilalama's successor, Isharramashu.

"Uṣurawasu, the ambassador (*kin-ge-a*) of Anumutabil, king of Der." Of this king we know just enough so that his appearance in our texts at this juncture in the history of Eshnunna is extremely significant; he headed a movement of reaction in which the south tried to rid itself of the foreigners. Now Anumutabil claims to have defeated Elam and its allies of the mountains.[1] We have seen that the disaster at Eshnunna after Bilalama's reign coincides with a dark period in Elam. It seems not too bold to suggest that Bilalama, or perhaps Isharramashu, allied with Elam, was defeated by Anumutabil, who installed in Eshnunna his own nominee Uṣurawasu, since the latter knew the country from having visited it as ambassador.

Anumutabil's action did not have any lasting results; in fact, it went straight against the course which events were taking. Yet it is remarkable that the two subsequent rulers, the first whose buildings are again of any importance at all, bear purely Sumerian names, Urninmar and Urningishzida. Urninmar must have been the earlier of the two. We have seen in chapter i that he first restored, and therefore must have lived some time in, the palace which was reconstructed on the ruins of the burned building, where his bricks occur alongside those of Isharramashu and Aṣuṣu. Whether either or both of these two are successors of Bilalama or of Uṣurawasu it is still impossible to say.[2] But after some time Urninmar heightened the site and built an entirely new palace. In this palace we find in at least one room two undisturbed thresholds, one with bricks of Urninmar and one with bricks of Urningishzida; elsewhere a drain of the latter overlies one of Urninmar. These two cannot, therefore, have been separated by any length of time. All the evidence suggests that Urninmar was the earlier. Each is styled *ishakku* on his bricks. But we know that Urninmar's son, Ibiq-Adad I, also ruled, though he was apparently preceded by Urningishzida. And we may well enumerate here some similarly strange facts which we shall meet farther on: though Ibiq-Adad I's son Dadusha became *ishakku* and Dadusha's son Ibalpel also ruled, yet another son of Ibiq-Adad I, namely, Naramsin, appears as ruler of Eshnunna.

Dr. Jacobsen has given a good deal of thought to the order of the numerous rulers who appear in our inscriptions—rulers to only seven

[1] The text was last published by Dr. Jacobsen in *American Journal of Semitic Languages and Literatures* XLIV (1927/28) 261.

[2] Cf. p. 32, n. 1.

or eight of whom can be ascribed a definite sequence of architectural remains. He now suggests that our view of the dependence of Kirikiri's dynasty on Elam may solve our puzzle satisfactorily, if we assume that the laws of succession in Elam and Eshnunna were the same. In Elam the old matriarchal order of society prevailed: at the death of a king all the sons of his mother had precedence over his children. After the death of the last of the dead king's brothers his own eldest son succeeded, after him his brothers, and so on. If Urningishzida were a brother of Urninmar, his accession to the throne before Ibiq-Adad I would be perfectly explicable on the basis of the Elamite system. The same principle would explain the accession of Dadusha's brother Naramsin before his son Ibalpel and perhaps even the place which the obscure Sharria seems to take as immediate successor of Ibalpel and the places of Abdiaraḫ and Shiqlanum as possible successors of Ibiq-Adad II (cf. p. 50). This hypothesis is extremely attractive because it does explain several otherwise incomprehensible facts. There is no more positive argument against it than the doubt whether such a system, which (as a well known adaptation of a matriarchal scheme to a world which needed male rulers) included brother-and-sister and son-and-mother marriages, could be taken from the soil in which it was rooted by primeval tradition and transplanted to another community. Even if we claim that the marriage of Bilalama's daughter with the king of Susa shows that he must have been of the blood royal of Elam, there remains the difficulty that Urninmar's dynasty is separated from that of Kirikiri by an interval during which we must assume that a dynastic break occurred and that a break with Elam was forced upon Eshnunna by Uṣurawasu; and out of this period of darkness emerge two rulers with Sumerian names. It is always possible that special circumstances, such as the absence of adult heirs in the direct line at times when a strong ruler was required, caused the succession of the late king's brother. We can but hope that further excavations may clear up the interrelations of these various rulers.

Whatever may have been the influence of Uṣurawasu at Eshnunna, good relations with Elam were certainly restored during the reign of Urninmar's dynasty. It was, in fact, unavoidable that a state which had its center of gravity beyond the Tigris should insure its safety by an alliance with the mountaineers beyond its eastern border. And when we find that Urninmar's grandson succeeds in extending his dominion as far west as the Euphrates, we must not forget that this rise of Eshnunna to power is parallel to a similar rise of the Elamite outposts in Babylonia under Kudurmabug. To the very last, until the final struggle for the hegemony in Babylonia between Kudurmabug's son Rimsin and Hammurabi, Eshnunna is found as an ally of the Elamites.

Of Naramsin, Urninmar's grandson, we know a great deal. He ruled Sippar, for a year in that city was dated after an event in his reign (cf. p. 26); and one of our tablets has a year date which may probably be read: "Year when Naramsin conquered Durbalati." This city, if the reading proves correct, is no doubt identical with the city of that name which according to the annals of Tukultininurta II of Assyria lay on the west bank of the Euphrates, two days' march north of Sippar and one day's march south of Rapiqu (cf. Fig. 1 and pp. 36–37).[1] Thus Naramsin's kingdom dominated both the route along the Tigris and that along the Euphrates. His brick inscription reflects his position. More elaborate than those in use before his day, it names his father also; and instead of styling himself *ishakku*, i.e., "governor" (namely, under the god) of Eshnunna, he calls himself "mighty king, king of Eshnunna" (cf. p. 47). Even his name seems to proclaim a policy. We know, moreover, that he was deified in his lifetime; and we may perhaps ascribe to him the deification of his father Ibiq-Adad I, who in his own inscriptions appears as a simple *ishakku* (but see p. 47).

We do not know whether Naramsin had a son; in any case his brother Dadusha appears as *ishakku* of Eshnunna on a weight found at Assur,[2] and a date formula on the Ishchali tablets mentions his accession. Dadusha was deified and carried the title of king, both of which facts would point to his having followed Naramsin. Neither of the brothers built in that part of the palace which we have exca-

[1] Luckenbill, *Ancient Records of Assyria and Babylonia* I (Chicago, 1926) § 408.

[2] *Keilschrifttexte aus Assur historischen Inhalts* (Leipzig, 1922) 2. Heft, No. 3. Dr. Jacobsen writes: "Schroeder restored *da-du-*[*um*] in the first line, but did not indicate it sufficiently plainly as a restoration in the heading and list of names. As a result of this, a fictitious "Dadum" occurs in *Cambridge Ancient History* I and elsewhere as a ruler of Eshnunna. The date formulas and the brick inscriptions of Ibalpel make it certain that we should restore *da-du-*[*sha*]."

vated so far; but as their father Ibiq-Adad had erected an entirely new and enlarged edifice above that of Urninmar, we may perhaps assume that it was the father who consolidated the interior position and organized the wealth of the country, which in the sons' reigns found its correlative in outward expansion.

Dadusha's son Ibalpel built again. Of the latter's son, Ibiq-Adad II, both Tell Asmar and other sources provide rather full information. In the first place the epithets are more elaborate than any earlier ones we have found: "Ibiq-Adad, mighty king, king who enlarges Eshnunna, shepherd of the black-headed (people), beloved of Tishpak, son of Ibalpel." Surely to such a one it is befitting to ascribe the feat for many years known from tablets in the British Museum and now also found in the date formulas of our own tablets: the capture of Rapiqu. While investigating the meaning of this achievement, we must at the same time consider another formula mentioning a conquest hardly less remarkable, that of Dur-rutumme(?), which Dr. Jacobsen suggests might be the Dur-rudumme mentioned by Sennacherib, situated almost in Babylonian territory. With Ibiq-Adad II the history of Eshnunna becomes clearly an essential part of the history of Babylonia.

In Babylonia Rimsin was still most powerful. Now that our excavations have located Eshnunna, which was known to be his ally, we are better able to understand his position: he dominated, either directly or, as in the case of Eshnunna, through allied princes, the whole long stretch of country between the Tigris on the west and the Elamite mountains and the Zagros range on the east. His dominion extended as far north as Assur, where he was acknowledged as king.[1] It is interesting that the inscribed stone weight given by Dadusha of Eshnunna to his daughter Inibsina was found at Assur, where she may have married the governor or some high official. Another connection between Assur and Eshnunna is evidenced by a letter (Tell Asmar 230, dating from before the conflagration) which, according to Dr. Jacobsen, clearly involves the application of old Assyrian laws.[2] But in the

[1] Cf. Gadd, *The Early Dynasties of Sumer and Akkad* (London, 1921), p. 35. The last doubts on the subject are removed by a consideration of the geographical conclusions which are given in our text as following from the identification of Eshnunna with Tell Asmar. See also Smith, *op. cit.* pp. 185–89.

[2] Dr. Jacobsen writes: "This letter was written by a young man who had been sold as a slave by some patricians with whom he lived. He wants to be set free,

south Rimsin's domain extended toward the west to include Larsa, which was protected by the marshland to the south of it.

In comparison Babylon's power was not impressive. In the 15th year of Rimsin's reign it attempted to break his power by a coalition with Larsa's neighbor Erech, with Isin, with Rapiqu, and with the Sutu (the equivalent of the modern Bedawin) who roamed the plains on the middle Euphrates. The confederates were defeated. Since, as the date formulas tell us, Rimsin's ally, Ibiq-Adad II of Eshnunna, subsequently took Rapiqu, we are now in a position to realize the menace which this implied for Babylon: Rapiqu dominated the passage over the Euphrates, as does its modern successor, Feluja, and thus formed the gate through which the "Amorite" dynasty of Babylon could call to its aid the nomads from its ancient homeland in the northwest. We have seen that the Sutu provided a contingent strong enough to be worth mentioning in Rimsin's formula. This gate to the northwest was closed, now that Rapiqu had fallen into the hands of Rimsin's ally. The wide-flung circle of Babylon's enemies began to close round that city. In fact, the conquest of Dur-rutumme by Ibiq-Adad brought war yet nearer to the city which Hammurabi was soon to deliver from the danger of imminent disaster.

But here, at the most fascinating point of our story, the sources run almost dry. We have found the traces of the building activity of Ibiq-Adad II at the very surface of the soil (see p. 12). We can state only that after his day there was no building of any extent on our palace site, but that he himself laid foundations for a large palace which, as we have seen, cut ruthlessly through older buildings. Bricks of one more ruler, Belakum, are found. He seems to have modified the palace in a few minor points. From tablets Dr. Jacobsen ingeniously concludes (see p. 50) that Ibiq-Adad II may have had two sons, Abdiaraḫ and Shiqlanum, the latter of whom at any rate became a ruler. He might be placed before Belakum.

For the last years of Eshnunna's independence we have thus at present only Hammurabi's year dates to guide us. It would be inter-

---

that he may prosecute those who sold him. The phraseology of the letter and the laws which it would seem to presuppose in Eshnunna at that time bear a striking resemblance to old Assyrian laws as preserved in Schroeder, *Keilschrifttexte aus Assur verschiedenen Inhalts* (Leipzig, 1920) No. 6, § 2, and may be explained on the assumption that both drew on pre-Hammurabi Akkadian laws."

esting to trace the stages by which he created for Babylon the position which that city was to retain for two millennia. Here it must suffice to state that we can distinguish two groups of campaigns. In the first half of his reign he staved off the most imminent danger. Here belongs, of course, the reopening of the road to the northwest; we find, indeed, that Rapiqu was captured in his 15th year. Then, after a period of consolidation and preparation, we can follow a carefully thought-out series of campaigns from his 29th year onward. First, a confederation of Rimsin's allies was met and defeated; Eshnunna, as usual, figured among these. In the next year Yamutbal was subjugated, and Rimsin himself was captured. This disposed of the most important adversary and pacified the countries on the southwest. The next year Eshnunna was conquered, as were Subartu and Gutium farther to the northeast. Herewith his authority was unquestionably established; when a flood, no doubt of the Diyala River, destroyed Eshnunna six years later, the country was considered so much a part of Hammurabi's domains that the year was named after the calamity. Strange to say, this event has left no trace at present discernible on the site where we are excavating, in contrast with some other less well dated floods in Babylonia of which much has been heard of late. It is obvious that we may hope for further light on this as on other problems connected with Hammurabi's war against Eshnunna.

As a matter of fact, it is only fair to state here explicitly that the details of the account given above are not all equally well supported by evidence, though the present writer considers this reconstruction most likely to reflect the actual course of events. But on some points we must hope for further elucidation. In the first place, it would be desirable to prove definitely that it was Ibiq-Adad II, and not the first ruler of that name, who conquered Rapiqu. The evidence on which we have relied is circumstantial. Rapiqu could not have become a member of a confederation hostile to Rimsin if it were in the power of Eshnunna; consequently it was free in Rimsin's 15th year. We assume that the victory of Rimsin over the confederation was either made easier by a simultaneous attack by his ally on Rapiqu, or that, on the contrary, Rimsin's victory created the possibility which Ibiq-Adad II subsequently used. The difference existing between the epithets of Ibiq-Adad II and those of all the other rulers justifies the assumption that he was a particularly successful conqueror. On the other hand, if we assign the date formulas on Rapiqu to Ibiq-Adad I, we have to assume in the first place that not Naramsin but Ibiq-Adad, who did not even call himself king, was the founder of the larger Eshnunna. This is possible, of course, but, after what we have said above, not likely. Secondly, we must assume that Rapiqu, independent again, had recovered far enough in the 15th year of Rimsin to take an active part in the war against him, which also sounds improbable. Moreover, this would imply that one of Ibiq-Adad I's successors lost Rapiqu. Though not impossible, for this too there is no evidence.

Our own material does not allow us to go any farther. But Mr. Sidney Smith has most generously supplied us with some evidence which seems to clinch the matter. On British Museum tablet No. 82438 (Bu. 91-5-9, 2480), dated in the "year that Ibiq-Adad . . . . ," the witnesses take the oath by Shamash, Ai, Marduk, and Hammurabi. There is, then, no possibility of doubt that the Ibiq-Adad who conquered Rapiqu was contemporary with Hammurabi; and the circumstantial evidence given above makes it more than probable that he was the second ruler of that name.

Though we are thus able to follow the history of Eshnunna with some precision through Ibiq-Adad II's reign, we have very little to go by for the succeeding years (cf. pp. 49-50). But we know already that more information concerning these later times may be expected from the continuation of our work, not so much at Tell Asmar as at other cities of Eshnunna the ruins of which fall within our concession. Tell Asmar, we believe, will teach us more about the ages preceding the period with which we have been dealing in this chapter.

KING LIST AND SYNOPSIS OF THE HISTORY OF ESHNUNNA AS REVEALED BY THE EXCAVATIONS

Year b.c.*	Babylonian Overlord	Ruler of Eshnunna	Events of the Reign
2247	Shulgi of Ur, year 29	Urguedinna	E-sikil was built by Shulgi for Ninazu or Tishpak
2231	year 45	Kallamu	Was probably transferred by his overlord from Kazallu to Eshnunna
2221–2213	Gimilsin of Ur	Ituria	Built temple to the god Gimilsin
2212–2187	Ibisin of Ur		
		Ilushuilia	Built palace adjoining temple of Gimilsin
		Nurakhum	Secularized palace chapel, but continued use of Gimilsin temple
2187	Ibisin captured for the Elamites by Ishbi-irra of Isin	Kirikiri	Probably had relations with Elamite rulers
		Bilalama	Rebuilt palace, discontinued use of Gimilsin temple; rebuilt E-sikil for Tishpak; extended his territory by alliance with Amorites; his daughter Mekubi married ruler of Susa
		Isharramashu	Palace was destroyed by fire, probably in course of anti-Elamite Sumerian campaigns of Anumutabil of Der
		Uṣurawasu	Was originally vassal of Anumutabil of Der
		Aṣuṣu ?	
		Urninmar	First reconstructed palace, then renewed it entirely
		Urningishzida ᵈIbiq-Adad I	Enlarged palace
		ᵈNaramsin	Conquered Sippar and probably Durbalati
		ᵈDadusha	Had relations with Assur; perhaps daughter married there
		Ibalpel	Rebuilt palace

* The absolute dates are taken from Weidner's list in Meissner, *Babylonien und Assyrien* II (Heidelberg, 1925) 439–52. These reigns are, however, dated about 120 or even 170 years earlier in various publications. Shulgi's building activity in Eshnunna and the positions of Ilushuilia and Nurakhum were revealed by discoveries during the second campaign at Eshnunna.

The rulers Sharria and Belakum may be successors to Ibalpel and Ibiq-Adad II respectively, but we do not yet have enough data to justify their inclusion in the king list.

KING LIST AND SYNOPSIS OF THE HISTORY OF ESHNUNNA AS REVEALED BY THE EXCAVATIONS—*Continued*

Year B.C.	Babylonian Overlord	Ruler of Eshnunna	Events of the Reign
About 1950		[d]Ibiq-Adad II	Conquered Rapiqu (between 1955 and 1940) and probably also Dur-rudumme; rebuilt palace
		Abdiaraḫ Shiqlanum	
1924	Hammurabi, year 31		Eshnunna was conquered by Hammurabi

III

DOCUMENTARY CONTRIBUTIONS TO THE HISTORY AND RELIGION OF ESHNUNNA

By THORKILD JACOBSEN

A SEAL INSCRIPTION OF KIRIKIRI

The oldest independent ruler of Eshnunna yet known to us is a man with the foreign-sounding name of Kirikiri. Our only written record from his time is a seal which he presented to his son Bilalama (Fig. 14). Dr. Frankfort has shown on page 27 that for archeological reasons Bilalama must be placed shortly after the fall of the 3d dynasty of Ur, and he thinks that "there is good reason to suppose that Kirikiri was .... founder of the dynasty of independent kings."

The inscription on Kirikiri's seal is particularly well cut; the signs are clear and without mistakes. It is therefore surprising to find that the Akkadian of the inscription is rather awkward and stands in strange contrast with the skill exhibited by the stonecutter.

The inscription runs:

^{d}*tišpak*	"(O) Tishpak,
šarrum da-núm	mighty king,
šàr ma-at wa-ri-im	king of the land of Warum!
ki-ri-ki-ri	Kirikiri,
išak	*ishakku*
áš-nun-na^{ki}	of Eshnunna,
a-na	to
bi-la-la-ma	Bilalama
DUMU.NI-*šu*	his son
i-qí₄-iš	has presented (this seal)."

The author of this inscription apparently did not know Sumerian, for he considered it necessary to add the Akkadian suffix -*šu*, "his," to the Sumerian DUMU.NI, which in itself means "his son." But even the Akkadian of the inscription is poor and does not give good sense. The first three lines stand completely isolated, without connection with what follows. Even if we consider them an address to Tishpak, as we have treated them in our translation, the result is not satisfactory, for such an address is out of place here.

The explanation of the peculiar wording of our inscription is probably that the inscription constitutes an inorganic mixture of two types of seal inscription. The first type, which we may call *a*, runs:

"O A! I, B, am your servant."

The second type, *b*,[1] runs:

"A to B, his servant (var., 'his son'), has presented (this seal)."

It is easy to see that the first three lines of Kirikiri's inscription are patterned after *a*; but instead of the natural continuation "I, B, am your servant," an inscription of type *b* has been added without regard to the sense of the whole.

The philological defects of the inscription, taken together with the foreign names of Kirikiri and his son, suggest that the kingdom of Eshnunna may have been founded by foreigners. However, as the proper names at Eshnunna do not show any conspicuous proportion of foreign elements during this period, it seems likely that only the ruling family and perhaps a small aristocracy had come from outside.

Of more than usual interest is the title "king of the land of Warum" which Kirikiri gives to Tishpak. According to the old Sumero-Akkadian theories of theocracy, the human ruler did not himself own the land over which he ruled. The local god was the owner, *lugal*, while the human ruler was only the god's feoffee, *isag*, who took care of the god's estate but did not own it himself.

Since the *ishakku* is the manager of the god's estate, we must a priori assume that the territory ruled by the *ishakku* is identical with the territory owned by the god. As in this case Kirikiri is *ishakku* of Eshnunna while Tishpak is king of the land of Warum, it is obvious that "the land of Warum" and "Eshnunna" are more or less synonymous terms; probably Eshnunna was the capital of the land of Warum, and the latter was the district around Eshnunna.[2] Further basis for

---

[1] Type *a* is so common that it is unnecessary to quote examples. On type *b* see Scheil in *Revue d'assyriologie* XXII (1925) 147–49, also Joint Expedition of the British Museum and of the Museum of the University of Pennsylvania to Mesopotamia, "Ur Excavations," *Texts* I (1928) "Royal Inscriptions" Nos. 88, 96, and 97.

[2] Outside the seal impressions from Eshnunna *mat warum* occurs in an unpublished text of Samsuiluna (Berlin VA 5951 ii 2–4) to which Dr. Falkenstein has called my attention. The passage is cited by Poebel, *Grundzüge der sumerischen Grammatik* (Rostock, 1923) § 376.

this assumption may be found in two seal inscriptions of Aṣuṣu, a later ruler of Eshnunna; for in one of them Tishpak is styled "king of the land of Warum,"[1] in the other, simply "king of Eshnunna."[2]

As for the name "Warum" itself, there can be little doubt that we have in it the Akkadian prototype of the Sumerian name for Akkad, which occurs in the form *uri* or *ari*.[3] The Akkadian *warum* was borrowed by the Sumerian in the genitive form *warim* because it was heard regularly in the standing phrase *mat warim*, "the land of Warum." As Sumerian has no *w*, the name would appear there in the forms *ari* and *uri*,[4] just as Akkadian *wardum*, "slave," was taken over by the Sumerians in the forms *arad* and *urdu*.[5] The final *m* would disappear in Sumerian after either *i* or *u*.[6]

In this connection it should be mentioned that Jensen as early as 1924, seven years before the form was actually found, saw that Sumerian *ari* and *uri* go back to an original form *wari*.[7] He also, and probably rightly, combined this word with Sumerian *ari*, "foe."

That the name of the district around Eshnunna should be identical with the old Sumerian term for northern Babylonia opens up interesting historical perspectives. As northern Babylonia was called Akkad because Agade was the most important kingdom in that region, it is possible that in still earlier times it was called *uri* because *mat warim* was the most important of its kingdoms. However, since we still know nothing about the earlier history of Eshnunna, it is wise not to draw any conclusions until pick and shovel have produced more tangible evidence.

[1] Tell Asmar 224.

[2] T.A. 310.

[3] Though the reading *uri* of sign No. 117 in Thureau-Dangin, *Recherches sur l'origine de l'écriture cunéiforme* (Paris, 1898) is attested when the sign stands for *akkadū* ("Akkadian"), the reading *ari* is as yet attested only when the sign stands for *amurrū* ("Amorite"). These two readings, however, are so similar that they cannot well be separated but must be variant pronunciations of the same geographical term.

[4] Deimel, *Šum. Lex.*, No. 359; G. Howardy, *Clavis cuneorum*, 7. Lfg. (1930) No. 342:5.

[5] Deimel, *op. cit.* No. 50:3.

[6] Cf. Poebel, *op. cit.* § 40.

[7] *Orientalistische Literaturzeitung* XXVII (1924) 61.

A BUILDING-INSCRIPTION OF BILALAMA

One of the year dates from the reign of Bilalama reads: "Year when Bilalama, *ishakku* of Eshnunna, built the E-sikil of Tishpak."[1] The event to which this formula refers, namely, the rebuilding of the temple called E-sikil, has been commemorated in a short inscription found on a few bricks from the palace also. Doubtless these bricks were originally meant for E-sikil, but were left over after its construction had been finished and were then used for other works.

The inscription mentioned runs:

a-na ᵈ*tišpak*	"For Tishpak
be-lí-šu	his lord
bi-la-la-ma	Bilalama,
na-ra-am-šu	his beloved
5 *ù na-áš-pár-šu*	and his envoy,
išak	ishakku
*áš-nun*ᵏⁱ	of Eshnunna,
é-sikil-am	E-sikil
ša i-ra-a-mu	which he loves
10 *ib-ni*	has built."[2]

The temple E-sikil which Bilalama built for Tishpak is the main temple of Eshnunna. It is mentioned outside the texts from Tell Asmar in a cycle of hymns to the chief temples of Babylonia recently published by Zimmern. One of the hymns in this cycle deals with E-sikil, the "house of Ninazu in Eshnunna."[3] The difficulties which arise from the fact that Bilalama's inscription assigns E-sikil to Tishpak, whereas the hymn considers it the temple of Ninazu, I have dealt with on pages 55–58.

The reading of the name as E-sikil is certain from another text in which this temple is mentioned, namely, the boundary stone of Nazimaruttash.[4] Though the name in the inscription of Bilalama could be read equally well *bītam el-am* or *é-sikil-am*, on the boundary stone it is written phonetically as *é-si-kil-la*, which decides in favor of the Sumerian rendering.

[1] Tell Asmar 350.

[2] T.A. 302.

[3] *Zeitschrift für Assyriologie* XXXIX (1930) 267 ff.

[4] Scheil, "Kudurru de Nazimaruttaš," iv 28, in "Mémoires de la Délegation en Perse" II (1900); Hinke, *Selected Babylonian Kudurru Inscriptions* (Leiden, 1911) pp. 1–4.

All of the titles of Bilalama are of a religious character, stressing the dependence of the ruler upon the city god. Bilalama is Tishpak's feoffee (*ishakku*), his envoy who deals with affairs in his stead. The reason why he occupies this high position is revealed by the title "his beloved": Tishpak approves of him and has therefore intrusted him with his earthly affairs.

The titles of the rulers of Eshnunna were apparently rather constant. A few, e.g., Naramsin, Dadusha, and Ibiq-Adad, change the pious *išakku*, "feoffee," for the more secular *šarru*, "king"; but all of them retain "beloved of Tishpak." When this title "beloved of the god so-and-so" originated we do not know; it goes back at least to Eannatum of Lagash, who calls himself "beloved of Dumuziabzi."[1] After relatively infrequent use among the Babylonian rulers, it became quite common under the 3d dynasty of Ur. It may, therefore, have been assumed by the dynasty of Kirikiri in imitation of the former overlords of Eshnunna.

The title "envoy of Tishpak" was also used by other rulers of Eshnunna, but not as regularly as "beloved of Tishpak." I know of only one occurrence of a similar title outside Eshnunna: Nabunaid once styles himself *našpar lā āneḫi*, "the untiring envoy."[2]

"GENEALOGICAL" BRICK INSCRIPTIONS

When it came to editing a brick inscription, the rulers of Eshnunna, or perhaps their scribes, were most conservative and, to the taste of the modern historian, rather unimaginative. Of the eleven rulers who have left us brick inscriptions, not less than ten use a short "standard inscription" of the type

"X, beloved of Tishpak, *ishakku* of Eshnunna."

So it happened that, although we found a considerable number of rulers' names in the course of our excavation, it was most difficult, sometimes almost hopeless, to ascertain their chronological order; for not all of these rulers could be placed by archeological evidence, as the bricks bearing the inscriptions were often found loose or in secondary use.

[1] Barton, *The Royal Inscriptions of Sumer and Akkad* I (New Haven, 1929) 32, No. 2 ii 8–9, and 36, No. 3 ii 11–12; Thureau-Dangin, *Die sumerischen und akkadischen Königsinschriften*, pp. 20 (A ii 8–9) and 22 (B ii 11–12).

[2] Langdon in "Vorderasiatische Bibliothek" IV (1912) 234, No. 3 i 9.

It was, therefore, most gratifying to discover one day, in close succession, two brick inscriptions of a different type—the longer inscriptions of Naramsin and Ibalpel.[1] To these was soon added the inscription of Ibiq-Adad II. As examples of this type—we called them "genealogical" bricks because the king mentions the name of his father—I give in transliteration and translation the inscriptions of Naramsin[2] and of Ibiq-Adad II.[3] The inscription of Ibalpel[4] is in every detail a true replica of that of Naramsin, except that the names are different and that neither Ibalpel nor his father Dadusha has the determinative for divinity in front of his name.

The oldest of the three inscriptions reads:

ᵈna-ra-am-ᵈE[N.ZU]	"Naramsin,
šarrum da-an-nu-um	mighty king,
šàr èš-nun-naᵏⁱ	king of Eshnunna,
na-ra-am ᵈtišpak	beloved of Tishpak,
mār ᵈi-bi-iq-ᵈadad	son of Ibiq-Adad."

The author of this inscription is, of course, Naramsin the younger, who was already known from a date formula on a tablet from Sippar.[5] No one, however, had suspected that he was a king of Eshnunna. It is noteworthy that both he and his father have been deified, as shown by the determinative for god in front of each name.

As far as we know, Ibiq-Adad I, the father of Naramsin, was the first ruler of Eshnunna to call himself a god.[6] Is it, then, a mere coincidence that he should call his son by the name Naramsin, the name of the first ruler of the dynasty of Agade who was deified? It seems to me much more natural to associate these two facts by assuming that

---

[1] This name is almost without exception written *i-ba-al-*PI*-el*. I have retained the old rendering Ibalpel although at this period PI generally stands for *wa, we*, which would give "Ibalwel," because we have two cases where the orthography *i-ba-al-bi-el* occurs (Tell Asmar 49 and Lutz, *Legal and Economic Documents from Ashjâly*, No. 44:17: [*i-b*]*a-al-bi-*[*el*]). Naturally this evidence is not of much importance, for, as we know, at this period the scribes did not distinguish clearly between *b* and *w*. The reading "Ibalpel" must therefore be considered purely provisional.

[2] T.A. 307.   [3] T.A. 312.   [4] T.A. 311.

[5] *Vorderasiatische Schriftdenkmäler* . . . . *Berlin* VIII (1909) No. 3; Schorr in "Vorderasiatische Bibliothek" V (1913) No. 213.

[6] But see p. 35, where the possibility that Naramsin deified his father has been envisaged.

the first Naramsin was the ideal of Ibiq-Adad I. After all, geographically the kingdom of Eshnunna in the latter's day included the kernel of the famous kingdom of Agade, so it would be no wonder if the rulers of Eshnunna considered themselves heirs to the proud traditions of Sargon and his successors.

The inscription of Ibiq-Adad II, which differs still more than that of Naramsin from the usual type, reads:

^{d}i-bi-iq-^{d}adad	"Ibiq-Adad,
šarrum da-núm	mighty king,
šarrum mu-ra-pí-iš	king who enlarges
èš-nun-na^{ki}	Eshnunna,
rē$^{\jmath}$u ṣa-al-ma-at	shepherd of
qá-qá-di-im	the black-headed (people),
na-ra-am ^{d}tišpak	beloved of Tishpak,
mār i-ba-al-pe-el	son of Ibalpel."

Several points in this inscription are of interest. First, we note that, although Ibiq-Adad writes with his own name the determinative of deity, he leaves his father Ibalpel an ordinary mortal. In this he seems to be fully in accord with the wishes of his predecessor, for Ibalpel does not in his own inscriptions use the divine determinative. Speaking of deification, we may add that Ibalpel's father Dadusha uses the determinative for deity in his own inscription,[1] whereas in the inscription of his son Ibalpel his name appears without the determinative. To sum up, we may say that the rulers of Eshnunna from Ibiq-Adad I down to Dadusha were deified, that Dadusha's son Ibalpel dispensed with the divine status and even refused it to his father, and that with Ibiq-Adad II, the son of Ibalpel, deification of the rulers again became customary.

This inconstancy in the assumption of deity may well be due to political reasons. Probably the powerful kingdom created by Ibiq-Adad I, which by its extent and importance entitled its ruler to call himself a god, suffered a reverse in the time of Dadusha, so that, although deified during the first part of his reign, that ruler had to give up the title and even his son Ibalpel never advanced beyond the status of an ordinary mortal. Since Dr. Frankfort has shown (p. 36) that Ibiq-Adad II succeeded in bringing important new territories under

[1] *Keilschrifttexte aus Assur historischen Inhalts*, 2. Heft, No. 3.

the sway of Eshnunna, it seems highly probable that it was this geographical expansion that enabled him to assume once more the proud symbol of deity used by his illustrious predecessors.

THE SUCCESSORS OF IBIQ-ADAD II

It is comparatively easy to determine the sequence of rulers of Eshnunna from Urninmar down to Ibiq-Adad II, because so many of them mention their fathers in their inscriptions. But with Ibiq-Adad II this state of affairs comes to an abrupt end, and far less precise sources are available.

In a vertical pottery drain sunk down through the remains of the palace many tablets were found. Their upper date limit may be fixed at approximately the time of Urninmar; their lower limit is still unknown to us. Two data formulas occurring here are: *mu ši-iq-la-nu-um ba-úš*, "year when Shiqlanum died,"[1] and *šattum ab-di-a-ra-aḫ* ᵈ*amurru-i-lí ri-di-šu i-pu-šu*, "year when Abdiaraḫ made Amurruili his successor."[2] The names Shiqlanum and Abdiaraḫ, the latter in the form Abdiraḫ,[3] occur together in the address of a letter found in the palace near the surface. The letter itself is unfortunately rather badly preserved and partly incrusted with salt; but the address, which is of particular interest to us here, is readable:

*a-na i-bi-iq-*ᵈ*adad*	"To Ibiq-Adad
qí-bí-ma	speak:
um-ma ab-di-ra-aḫ	Thus (say) Abdiraḫ
ù ši-iq-la-nu-um-ma	and Shiqlanum."[4]

That not only the addressee, Ibiq-Adad, but also the two authors of this letter have names borne by *ishakkus* of Eshnunna can scarcely be accidental, especially when we realize that the names Abdiraḫ and Shiqlanum, at least, are by no means common. It seems, therefore, probable that Abdiraḫ and Shiqlanum of the letter are identical with the *ishakkus* Abdiaraḫ and Shiqlanum whom we know from the date formulas quoted above. The Ibiq-Adad to whom they write may well

[1] Tell Asmar 231.

[2] T.A. 234.

[3] This name, which means "servant of the moon-god," occurs in the forms Abdiaraḫ, Abdiraḫ, and Ḫabdiaraḫ. See the material collected by Theo Bauer, *Die Ostkanaanäer* (Leipzig, 1926) p. 9.

[4] T.A. 2.

be Ibiq-Adad II. Ibiq-Adad I is out of the question, because we know who his successors were. The letter would then have been written while Abdiaraḫ and Shiqlanum were still young princes at the court of Ibiq-Adad II.

If we adopt the identification proposed above, it follows from the date formulas that both Abdiaraḫ and Shiqlanum succeeded to the throne. Which ruled first? The fact that Abdiraḫ is mentioned first in the letter seems to indicate that he was the more important. We may, therefore, in the absence of more precise information, assume that he was the nearer to the throne and succeeded Ibiq-Adad II. Since Shiqlanum eventually became a ruler of Eshnunna, we may conclude that he also had a claim to the throne. The nature of his claim we do not know; at least it was not respected by Abdiaraḫ, for the date formula informs us that he named Amurruili as his successor.

We have no evidence that Amurruili ever ruled Eshnunna. This may well have been due to Shiqlanum, who—so we may suppose—would defend his claim by force. As a matter of fact, we possess a tiny fragment of a tablet which with a little good will could be interpreted as evidence of a civil war in the time of Shiqlanum. The fragment runs:

. . . .	"[The regiment(?)]
⸢ša⸣ it-t[i . . . .]	which with . . . .
wa-aš-ba-at	is stationed
uš-te-ṣi-a[m]	he has led out.
um-ma šu-ú-ma	Thus (says) he:
ka-ki a-li-qí-ma	'I shall take my weapon;
it-ti ᵐši-iq-la-nim	with Shiqlanum
am-ta-ḫa-aṣ	I shall fight!'
. . . .	. . . ."[1]

If we are right in assuming a civil war, Shiqlanum must have come out victor, for we know that he became a ruler of Eshnunna.

We may then, *although with due reserve,* set up the following provisional order:

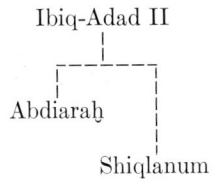

```
            Ibiq-Adad II
                 |
         ┌───────┴───────┐
         |               |
      Abdiaraḫ           |
                         |
                     Shiqlanum
```

[1] T.A. 189.

THE CHIEF GOD OF ESHNUNNA[1]

According to a Babylonian list of deities, the lord of Eshnunna was Tishpak.[2] This statement is corroborated by brick inscriptions found on the actual site of the city, for in these the *ishakkus* of Eshnunna invariably style themselves *naram tišpak*, "beloved of Tishpak."[3]

Although Tishpak[4] was included as a Babylonian god in the famous AN:*Anum* list of gods, his name is so thoroughly un-Babylonian that he must be of foreign origin. To ascertain his original home we must therefore turn to the foreign countries which in antiquity were the neighbors of Babylonia and try to link up the name Tishpak with the language of one or more of those countries.

When we look at the name Tishpak from this point of view, our attention is immediately drawn to the ending -*ak*, which has been compared with the similar ending -*ak* in the names of the Elamite gods Inshushinak and Dagbak. Some scholars have even gone so far as to identify it with the Elamite affix -*ak*[5] used with personal nouns in the singular; but as this Elamite affix seems to mean originally "I am,"[6] I do not see how it could become an integral part of a divine name. Even if we restrict our comparison to the -*ak* of Inshushinak and Dagbak and on that basis assume an Elamite origin for Tishpak, we get into difficulties. For if Tishpak were originally Elamite, we should be confronted with the strange fact that no traces of him survive in the Elamite pantheon.

But it is not necessary to go as far as Elam to find parallels to the ending -*ak* of Tishpak. Among the proper names occurring in early

---

[1] This paper was read at the 18th International Congress of Orientalists, held at Leyden in September, 1931.

[2] Rawlinson, *The Cuneiform Inscriptions of Western Asia* II (London, 1866) Pl. 60, No. 1:5a+4b.

[3] See Thureau-Dangin, *Die sumerischen und akkadischen Königsinschriften* (Leipzig, 1907) p. 174 (xvi 2–5), and compare our p. 46; see also the phrase ᵈ*tišpak ù eš-nun-na*ᵏⁱ *ša-lim*, "All is well with Tishpak and Eshnunna" (Lutz in "Yale Oriental Series. Babylonian Texts" II [1917] No. 143:6).

[4] Meissner, *Babylonien und Assyrien* II (Heidelberg, 1925) 35.

[5] Speiser (*Mesopotamian Origins* [Philadelphia and London, 1930] pp. 40–42 and 122) does not differentiate between the -*ak* affixed to personal or geographical names and the -*ak* of such divine names as Inshushinak.

[6] Cf. Bork, *Reallexikon der Vorgeschichte* III (1925) 74–75.

Babylonian documents are several which end in -*akum:* Belakum, Irḫakum, Izakum, Pallakum, Pappakum,[1] Shugakum, and Zanakum.[2] Now this type is well attested at Eshnunna itself; for one of its rulers bore the name Belakum, while persons called Bukakum, Dammamakum, and Sukakum occur in texts found at the site.[3] We have here, then, in Eshnunna itself, an ending -*akum* which is used as a formative element in proper names. It would be unnatural not to compare the ending of the divine name Tishpak or Tishpakum (as we may suppose the older form of the name was) with this -*akum* of the personal names. So we should probably explain the ending -*ak* of Tishpak as a local development.

Assigning the -*ak* of Tishpak to a local origin does not help us in our search for the original home of the god. But if we omit the ending -*ak*, there remains a stem *tishp*- which is almost identical with the stem of the name Teshup-ash belonging to the national god of the Ḫurrians. The disappearance of the vowel *u* is easily accounted for if we assume that the stress was on the first syllable, for Téshupak would become Téshpak, Tishpak.

As far as names are concerned, then, Tishpak may be identified with Teshup.[4] Can a similar identity be established between the characters of the two gods? If so, I believe we should be justified in regarding them as originally one. Since the character of Teshup as a god of thunderstorms is comparatively well known,[5] I shall deal chiefly

[1] For these names see Theo Bauer, *Die Ostkanaanäer*, p. 57.

[2] For *za-na-kum* see Schneider, *Orientalia* No. 23 (1927) p. 107, No. 1470; for *šu-ga-kum* see ibid. p. 184, No. 2673. Compare *sugagi, sugagum* in Ranke, *Early Babylonian Personal Names* (Philadelphia, 1905) p. 166.

[3] *Su-ga-kum, su-ka-kum*, Tell Asmar 10, 56, and 80; *bu-ga-ku-um, dam-ma-ma-kum*, T.A. 359 and 358.

[4] After I had finished this article I discovered that Hommel, *Grundriss der Geographie und Geschichte des alten Orients* (München, 1904) p. 39, n. 2, also mentions the possibility that Tishpak and Teshup are identical. The way he attacks the problem—dividing *tišpak* into *te* and *šipak* and identifying the latter element with the name of the Kassite god Shipak—is, however, not very well suited to furthering its solution. He says: ". . . . Tišpak wird wohl nur ein Kompos. aus *te* 'Herr' und *Šipak* sein, wie *te-isba-s* ein solches aus *te* und *isba*. Dass Tišpak (bezw. Šipak) und der mitannisch-vannische Teïsbas ganz zu trennen seien, dürfte doch wohl kaum anzunehmen sein."

[5] See Deimel, *Pantheon Babylonicum* (Rome, 1914) No. 3258; Meissner, *op. cit.* II 22.

with the character of Tishpak, which, if we may trust our material, was most complicated.

In the first place, Tishpak is sometimes identified with Ninurta as a god of ritual washings.[1] This is in harmony with the fact that his statue in Assur stood near a well.[2] But Tishpak was also a god of craftsmen, for he is identified once with Nabu[3] and once with Marduk[4] as god of craftsmen. From date formulas from Eshnunna we learn, moreover, that Tishpak had a "new-moon emblem set with silver."[5] The inference from this that he had some connection with the new moon could be supported by evidence from proper names such as Nur-ᵈTishpak, "Tishpak is light."[6] These different sides of Tishpak's character—god of ritual washings, god of craftsmen, and moon-god—are not easy to combine into a homogeneous picture, nor do they bear on traits which he might have in common with Teshup.

One important source, however, remains unmentioned, namely, the myth of Labbu, in which Tishpak plays a leading rôle.[7] According to this myth, the noise made by human beings prevents Enlil from sleeping.[8] He creates, therefore, an enormous serpent, Labbu, which is evidently intended to destroy them. But even the gods are affrighted; they crouch in heaven before Sin, asking him who shall go to kill Labbu. Sin asks Tishpak to undertake the task; but the latter declines, apparently on the ground that he does not know how to go

---

[1] *Cuneiform Texts* XXIV (1908) Pl. 41:64; XXV (1909) Pl. 11:29.

[2] *Keilschrifttexte aus Assur verschiedenen Inhalts* (Leipzig, 1920) No. 42 i 28 f.

[3] *Keilschrifttexte aus Assur religiösen Inhalts*, No. 94 i 50.

[4] *Cuneiform Texts* XXV, Pl. 50: obv. 11.

[5] T.A. 59.

[6] T.A. 231; cf. also ᵈtišpak-nu-ri, "Tishpak is my light," in T.A. 358.

[7] Jensen in "Keilinschriftliche Bibliothek" VI, 1. Teil (Berlin, 1900) 44–47.

[8] The opening lines of the myth are rather difficult. The explanation given above has been based upon the analogy to the Ea and Atraḫasis myth, in which Enlil—according to the ingenious reading of Sidney Smith (*Revue d'assyriologie* XXII [1925] 67)—wants to destroy the race of men because he cannot stand their noise. The same motive causes Tiamat to undertake the war against the younger gods. In the myth about Labbu we may have to restore lines 3–4 thus: ³a-na iq-qil-li-ši-na ul [. . . . ᵈEn-lil] ⁴a-na rim-ma-ti-ši-na ul i-ṣab-[bat-su šit-tu], "Because of their noise Enlil cannot . . . . ; because of their roaring he cannot sleep." That the text uses *ana* is probably because sleeplessness is considered a psychic state, and *ana* often introduces causes of psychic states. See Bezold, *Babylonisch-assyrisches Glossar* (Heidelberg, 1926) p. 45, No. 7.

about it. So Sin advises him to make a cloud ascend, to raise a storm, and then to throw his "seal of the throat" down upon Labbu. This "seal of the throat," which has been explained in various ways, is probably merely Tishpak's cylinder seal, described as "of the throat" because cylinder seals were usually worn on a string around the neck, the cylinder hanging in front of the throat. Tishpak follows the advice of Sin and succeeds in killing Labbu.

Now the Tishpak of this myth is a god who can raise storms and clouds, from which he throws down his cylinder seal to kill. There can be no doubt that such a god is a god of thunderstorms and lightning. The cylinder seal which Tishpak throws is evidently a primitive explanation of lightning, a belief for which numerous parallels could be quoted, for many primitive peoples consider lightning as a stone thrown down by the god of thunder. It follows, then, that both Tishpak and Teshup are gods of thunderstorms, hence identical in character as they were identical in name. I believe, therefore, that Tishpak is only a local form of Teshup.

The identification of Tishpak with Teshup has solved one problem, only to raise a number of new ones. For example, the examination of Tishpak's character has shown us numerous facets; he had many functions besides that of a god of thunder. Are we justified, then, in considering this function the original one;[1] and, if so, how did he acquire the others? Such questions are easier to put forth than to answer. I should think, however, that we are justified in considering Tishpak originally a god of thunderstorms, for we have found this characteristic in a myth which I have no doubt was originally a cult myth mimed at some annual festival of Tishpak's. In such a cult myth we should expect to find a true and original picture of the nature of the god.

The other question, how Tishpak, a god of thunderstorms, came to possess his many other functions, is more difficult. As a matter of fact, I do not believe it can be solved until more material is at our disposal. At present it is, at most, possible to indicate the direction from

[1] Some scholars would call it dangerous to prefer the evidence from a myth to that from the identifications, which evidently reflect the god as he appeared in the cult. In this special case, however, the cult seems to be a less safe indicator because, as I shall show later, there is a strong probability that the Tishpak cult which we meet in Eshnunna contains heterogeneous elements.

which the answer is probably to be sought. But this leads to a third and most important problem raised by the identification of Tishpak with Teshup. If Tishpak is ultimately a form of the Hurrian god Teshup, how did he become the city god of Eshnunna? Is he original there; or did he penetrate later, perhaps superseding an earlier divinity?

Before we can enter into this problem, we must turn for a moment to another god who has a rival claim to the position of chief god of Eshnunna. The main temple of Eshnunna, the abode of Tishpak, is mentioned in a brick inscription of Bilalama (cf. p. 45): "For Tishpak his lord Bilalama, his beloved and his envoy, *ishakku* of Eshnunna, E-sikil which he loves has built."

From this inscription we gather that the temple of Tishpak in Eshnunna was E-sikil. This same temple is mentioned in a Sumerian text from Nippur, recently published by Zimmern,[1] which contains a collection of old Sumerian hymns to the main temples of Babylonia. In the section which deals with E-sikil[2] the temple is ascribed not, as we should expect, to Tishpak, but to the god Ninazu, who is there described chiefly as a god of war. The last lines of that section read: "Great lord, with whose exalted splendid advance none can keep pace, legitimately engendered by the 'great mountain' (i.e., Enlil) and Ninlil! (O) E-sikil, thy king, the warrior Ninazu, has placed a house in thy territory(?); in thy cella he has taken up his residence." Then follows a subscript: "The house of Ninazu in Eshnun."[3]

The god Ninazu whom we meet here as lord of E-sikil is a little better known to us than is Tishpak. As stated in the hymn just mentioned, Ninazu's parents were Enlil and Ninlil. In archaic Sumerian texts we find him as the spouse of Ereshkigal[4] the queen of Hades, and it is likely that he and she together ruled "the land of no return." In later times, however, he was superseded by Nergal. In the AN:*Anum* list his wife is a certain Ningirda.[5] Ningishzida was their son.[6] Outside Eshnunna Ninazu was worshiped in the city of IM.KI

[1] *Zeitschrift für Assyriologie* XXXIX (1930) 245–76.
[2] *Ibid.* pp. 267–68.
[3] *Ibid.* p. 268.
[4] Deimel, *Pantheon Babylonicum*, No. 2406; Meissner, *op. cit.* II 34, n. 19.
[5] Meissner, *op. cit.* II 34.   [6] *Ibid.* p. 34.

(perhaps to be read as Muru) in southern Mesopotamia.[1] That Ninazu is a chthonic god is clear, not only because he is regularly listed with the infernal deities,[2] but also from his marital relations with Ereshkigal the queen of Hades. In the hymn quoted above he is depicted as a god of war and destruction.

The rival claims of Tishpak and Ninazu to the lordship of E-sikil and of Eshnunna raise the question of priority. The first thing to be looked into in this connection is the age of Zimmern's text, or rather of the tradition upon which it is based. The text itself gives us a clue, for in the colophon it mentions a king named En-ḫé-du₇-an-na as its author. As Zimmern points out,[3] this king may perhaps be identical with En-úg(?)-du-an-na, the first king of the 2d dynasty of Uruk. If this identification is right—and it seems to me highly probable—Sumerian tradition places the origin of the composition in a very remote age. Such a tradition is supported by the completely Sumerian outlook of the text, another feature noted by Zimmern: the cities mentioned are all old Sumerian centers; foreign gods such as MAR.TU and Ishḫara who were later included in the pantheon are completely absent. High age is indicated again by the close relation between Ninazu and Ereshkigal which the text presupposes in the section on Ninazu as the god of Muru, for we have Ninazu as the husband of Ereshkigal in archaic times only. In the section on Nergal of Kutha, who later superseded Ninazu as the husband of Ereshkigal, our text does not mention Ereshkigal at all.

Though all these features favor confidence in the Sumerian tradition, there is one circumstance that would seem completely to exclude an early date for the text. One of the hymns is addressed to the temple of Shulgianna, who, as Zimmern rightly points out, is no other than the deified king Shulgi of the 3d dynasty of Ur.[4] This section, therefore, cannot be older than Shulgi's own time; but does that hold for the whole composition?

We know that the Sumerians not infrequently inserted new sec-

---

[1] Zimmern, *Zeitschrift für Assyriologie* XXXIX (1930) 257; Legrain, *Historical Fragments* (Philadelphia, 1922) No. 41: rev. 1.

[2] Meissner, *op. cit.* II 34.

[3] *Zeitschrift für Assyriologie* XXXIX (1930) 249.

[4] *Ibid.* p. 254.

tions into old compositions in order to bring them up to date. May not the hymn to Shulgianna's E-ḫursag be such an insertion? If so, it can have no value for dating the composition as a whole. By a lucky chance we are in position to prove that this is actually the case. In the last line of the Shulgi section, just before the subscript, we read the Akkadian word *taḫ-ḫu-um*. Though Zimmern translated the word as "substitute," following Ungnad,[1] he admits the unsuitability of that idea in our passage.

Now the word *taḫḫum*, which is a loan word from Sumerian TAḪ, is used in early Babylonian texts to designate a certain class of soldiers. But the usual translation, "substitutes," cannot be right; for we find that the TAḪ troops form companies with their own captains,[2] and in at least one instance a man and his TAḪ go to work together.[3] In both these cases the translation "substitute" will not work; on the other hand there is good evidence in favor of translating as "reserve." Since the Sumerian word TAḪ really means "to add," the Sumerians probably thought of the reserve as an "additional force." This explanation is strongly supported by the term applied to the class of soldiers which in the military rolls follows the TAḪ in rank, namely, the DIRIG, the "surplus."[4] *Taḫḫum*, therefore, like its Sumerian prototype TAḪ, in all probability means "addition"; and this translation gives excellent sense in the passage with which we are concerned. Whereas the other hymns have subscripts such as "House of Nanna in Ur" or "House of Innanna in Ḫallaba," this special hymn is designated as "Addition: E-ḫursag of Shulgi(anna) in Ur."[5]

But if this hymn is an "addition," it does not interfere with the dating of the composition itself, for which, as we have seen, there is not only the Sumerian tradition but also internal evidence in the text itself. From this it appears that we have good old tradition for Ninazu as the chief god of Eshnunna, a fact that weighs heavily in determining which of the two, Tishpak or Ninazu, is the earlier. We

[1] *Zeitschrift für Assyriologie* XXXI (1917/18) 56–57.
[2] Ungnad in "Vorderasiatische Bibliothek" VI (1914) No. 77.
[3] *Ibid.* No. 35.
[4] Unpublished military rolls from Khafaje, now in Chicago.
[5] Note also (*Zeitschrift für Assyriologie* XXXIX 254) the writing *urik'-a*, "in Ur," in the subscript of this section, as compared with *urikⁱ-ma*, "in Ur," in the section on the temple of Nanna.

should consider also the fact that the name of the disputed temple is purely Sumerian; certainly, if the Ḫurrian Tishpak were original there, he would not have lived, as he apparently did, in a Sumerian temple.

However, this is not all the evidence in favor of Ninazu. At Tell Asmar some clay tablets dating from about the time of the Isin dynasty were unearthed. On several of these tablets are mentioned offerings to the various gods worshiped in Eshnunna. One of those most frequently mentioned is Ningishzida, the son of Ninazu. How the son of Ninazu could come to be worshiped in a city belonging to Tishpak might still be explained; but when we find Tishpak coupled not only with Ningishzida, the son of Ninazu, but also with Enlil, the father of Ninazu, we are forced to admit that Tishpak is definitely surrounded by a Ninazu milieu. This is exactly the case in a tablet which enumerates offerings "for the house of Tishpak, for Ningishzida, and for Enlil."[1]

The fact that in Eshnunna Tishpak is surrounded by a Ninazu milieu permits, to my mind, only one explanation, namely, that Ninazu was the original god of Eshnunna and of E-sikil, where he was worshiped together with his family. Later,[2] Tishpak invaded the city and usurped the position of Ninazu, leaving more or less undisturbed, however, the routine of the cult and the worship of the minor deities who constituted Ninazu's family.

That the invading cult of Tishpak only partially supplanted the worship of Ninazu is suggested by the puzzling composite character of Tishpak. May not Tishpak's function as god of ritual washings, for example, have been a heritage from Ninazu?[3] Unluckily, our scanty knowledge of Ninazu's character does not permit us to decide the question; but there are several indications that he did have something to do with water. Meissner translates his name, *nin-a-zu*, as "der Wasserkundige"; and his name is found grouped with that of

[1] T.A. 43.

[2] Hardly after the dynasty of Agade, for the personal name Tishpakkum occurs on an unpublished tablet (now in Chicago) from this period.

[3] I consider as an almost certain case of influence by Ninazu on Tishpak the faint chthonic traits which we find in the latter. He is grouped with the chthonic gods in the AN:*Anum* list, and he occurs in Rawlinson, *loc. cit.*, which according to Ebeling (*Tod und Leben nach den Vorstellungen der Babylonier*, 1. Teil [Berlin and Leipzig, 1931] p. 9) is a list of chthonic deities.

Ninaḫakuddu,[1] "the lady of the washbasin." Further discoveries may clear up this point.

We may now sum up our results. The chief god of Eshnunna was at first the Sumerian Ninazu, a chthonic god who resided in the temple called E-sikil. Ninazu was later displaced by the Ḫurrian god Teshup, whose name at Eshnunna was changed to Tishpak by the addition of the element -*akum*. Tishpak took over E-sikil from Ninazu, but left the minor cults more or less undisturbed. As the chief god of an old Sumerian center, he succeeded finally in making his way into the official Babylonian pantheon as represented by the AN:*Anum* list,[2] where he follows almost directly his predecessor in Eshnunna, Ninazu.[3]

[1] Zimmern, *Beiträge zur Kenntnis der babylonischen Religion* (Leipzig, 1901) p. 40, *Šurpu* viii 4.

[2] Cf. Meissner, *op. cit.* II 2.

[3] Cf. *ibid.* pp. 34–35 and the literature there cited. A Sumerian list in the Louvre (AO. 5376 ix 15–20) likewise names Tishpak after the Ninazu group. It was first published by Genouillac in *Revue d'assyriologie* XX (1923) 89–106 and has since appeared in his *Textes religieux sumériens du Louvre* I ("Textes cunéiformes" XV [1930]) No. 10 (see his Plate XXX, lines 400–405). But Tishpak precedes Ninazu in a school list edited by Weidner (*Archiv für Keilschriftforschung* II [1924–25] 11) and again in *Šurpu* viii 4.

IV

KHAFAJE

By CONRAD PREUSSER

The results of the first campaign at Khafaje, a site some 15 kilometers east of Baghdad, are reported here rather fully, as I shall not return to the work. Final publication of the objects found will come later. The few which can be published here will suffice to show that in Khafaje we have struck an important source of new and rich information regarding the history of Sumer.

The work was started at the end of October, 1930, with the building of the expedition house. The actual excavation on Mound A, which began November 22 and was carried on with fifty men at an average, terminated March 3, 1931. While the house was being built, the survey of the site was also begun. My collaborators were my wife and Mr. Hamilton D. Darby, who as architect was responsible for the drawings. To their devotion to our common task are due the results which we can now publish.

Since the ancient name of Khafaje is not yet known, we must use the modern Arabic name till the soil which we are exploring yields the secret. The history of the site is equally unknown, as no inscriptions have been found. Possibly it was a provincial town belonging to the kings of Eshnunna, of whom, however, no remains have yet appeared.

THE SITE

Our plan of Khafaje (Fig. 19) is derived from a tachymetric survey on the scale 1:2000, based on the highest four points found among the ruins. These points were fixed by measuring the angles and were checked by double steel-tape measurements. The area was then divided into 100-meter squares oriented toward the magnetic north and designated as 1–19 from north to south and a–m from west to east. Each of these units was subdivided into 20-meter squares. A baked brick fixed in the wall of a circular basin in i B/9 IV was taken as main level point and was arbitrarily given an elevation of +40 meters.

The plan shows that the town consists of three apparently unconnected mounds. They are very low and merge very gradually into the plain. This is especially true of the spur northwest of Mound A. Point A itself rises only 3.75 meters above the lowest part of the plain. The highest point is at B (5.60 meters). Around and among the mounds extend fields watered by canals. Nowhere on the surface are traces of fortifications visible. But between the two southern mounds a clay embankment extends southeasterly from e/15 and joins beyond the modern canal the domelike hillock in g/16–17. After rain, brickwork can be seen which evidently belonged to a thick wall.

Arabs have dug for antiquities all over the ruins, but especially on the east slope of Mound B, on the west slope of A, and with appalling thoroughness on the north slope of A. On the plan, their pits are indicated by irregular black dots. To judge from the sherds etc. lying about on the surface, the ruins covered by Mounds B, C, and D would date from about the period of Hammurabi. Mound A, including its northwest spur, is older; for one finds there besides plano-convex bricks pottery similar to that of Fara and of Kish Cemetery A. In the northwest corner of g/7 we found several pieces of baked clay with reed impressions.[1] An extensive inclosure wall of plano-convex bricks is clearly visible in g–h/6. In only one spot (h A/5 III) there lay on the surface a few well baked but unfortunately uninscribed bricks, the whole ones measuring .38×.38×.07 and the halves .38×.18×.07. These belong to a later period.

What the plain between Mounds A and B contains remains unknown. There are neither sherds nor bricks lying about. Yet when we made a trench 1 meter wide by 8.50 meters deep to investigate this part of the site before putting our dump there, we found enough still undatable potsherds, slightly arched plano-convex bricks, animal bones, charred wood, and other evidences of human habitation to convince us that down to even greater depths much of interest and value might be discovered.

On account of its age Mound A seemed most suitable for the first investigation. We avoided penetrating into the deeper layers, as we wished first to lay bare the plan of the latest ruins; even these were

[1] Similar pieces were found in House D also. See pp. 91 and 94.

so old that they were built exclusively with plano-convex bricks.[1] Walls of this type actually reach the surface; sometimes only a few bricks remain, and occasionally even these last traces have been worn away or destroyed by illicit digging.

PLANO-CONVEX BRICKWORK

A few words must be said about the method of building with plano-convex bricks. As nowadays, the bricks were made of clay from the plain of the Two Rivers mixed with chopped straw to make them more durable. The mixture was pressed by hand into a wooden frame .03 or more high. The top was not smoothed off but was left with a camber of .03 or less. Usually a depression was made with the thumb to give the mud mortar a better grip. Many bricks show impressions of the fingers also. After removal of the frame the bricks were dried in the sun. Their average size was .15×.21×.03–.06.

These plano-convex bricks were laid diagonally and flat (Fig. 20), as we could observe in walls of the later period. Most frequently three diagonally laid courses, either in herringbone pattern (which could not, however, be seen in the finished walls, as it was covered with mud plaster) or all leaning in one direction, alternate with two or three courses of bricks laid flat with their convex sides up. These flat layers serve to equalize the unevenness of the diagonally laid courses and therefore act as a rather imperfect bonding. Bonding as we understand it was completely unknown to earlier builders of plano-convex brick structures, who built quite without rules and used no diagonally laid courses. Even the later attempt at bonding could not be wholly successful, as exact building with bricks of such a shape was impossible. One had to rely on the cohesive strength of the mortar, which consisted of the same material as the bricks themselves and formed together with these one strong homogeneous mass. Such a

[1] Plano-convex bricks found at Ur belong to the 1st dynasty (Woolley in *Antiquaries Journal* VIII [1928] 434). Other sites at which they have been found are al-ᶜUbaid (Hall and Woolley, *Al-ᶜUbaid* [Oxford, 1927] p. 66), Lagash (De Sarzec, *Découvertes en Chaldée* II [Paris, 1884–1912] Pls. 57 and 57 *bis*), Bismaya (Banks, *Bismya* [New York, 1912] p. 236), Nippur (Fisher, *Excavations at Nippur* [Philadelphia, 1905] pp. 21 ff.), Fara (Heinrich and Andrae, *Fara* [Berlin, 1931] pp. 8 ff.), Kish (Field Museum of Natural History, "Anthropology Memoirs" I [Chicago, 1925–31] 84 ff.), and Warka (Jordan, *Kurzbericht über Uruk 1930/31*, pp. 14 ff.).

mass does, indeed, become so hard that it is often impossible to disengage from it single bricks to take measurements.

Burned bricks were comparatively rare. They were used only when absolutely necessary, namely, in constructions such as drains and basins, where the brickwork came in contact with water, or in connection with floors (cf. p. 101). Obviously, burned brick was a costly material. Sizes varied considerably, but were in general similar to those of the unbaked bricks; the owners of kilns probably all used their own individual molds. There were sometimes one, sometimes two, im-

FIG. 20.—A circular brick construction

pressions of fingers. Most common was the size .15×.28×.03–.06. Sometimes the shape was trapezoid, in which case one of the short sides would measure only .12–.13; such bricks usually had one finger impression in the middle. The largest bricks had no finger impressions and measured .17×.32–.335×.05–.08. Within these limits, however, the variations were numerous. In the court of House D, for instance, the twenty-two bricks measured were all different in size. Their only common feature was a camber not exceeding .015.

THE EXCAVATIONS

A trial trench 5 meters wide, begun in k C/9 V at a spot relatively free from robbers' pits, was extended west-northwest to i E/9 IV. At

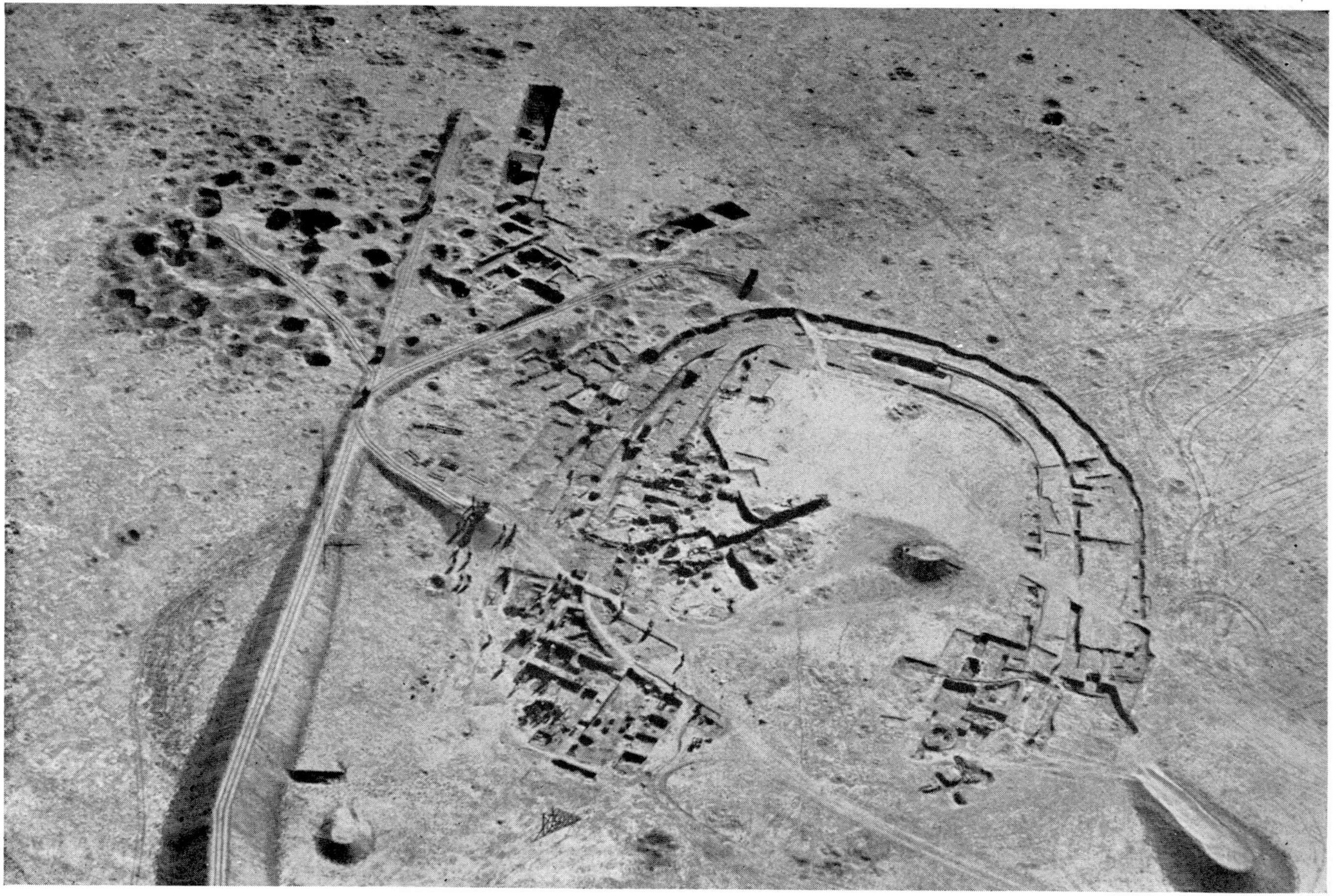

Fig. 21.—Air photograph of Khafaje

Crown Copyright Reserved *Royal Air Force Official*

its beginning the trench cut through upper layers without buildings but with old graves. In its western half, house foundations were discovered. Another trial trench on the western slope of the mound passed first through soil much disturbed by illicit digging, then struck walls over 3 meters thick which obviously belonged to monumental buildings. We felt obliged therefore to follow these and to make their excavation the main object of our campaign. Our expectations were realized as we gradually laid bare a very remarkable building (Figs. 21–22) for which no Sumerian parallel is yet known.

The results of the excavations may be summarized as follows. Two inclosure walls (the outer one provided with towers) surround an oval space of about 74×54 meters. Toward the west our investigation is not yet complete. The distance between the two walls is about 3 meters except on the north, where House D is included between the walls. This house and the outer wall at this point are evidently later. Outside of this self-contained unit there lie to the east on the mound still later town dwellings which extend down the slope and abut on the outer inclosure wall.

THE INCLOSURE WALLS

Within an average depth of about 1.40 meters, we have already been able to distinguish various building periods (Fig. 23). The oldest

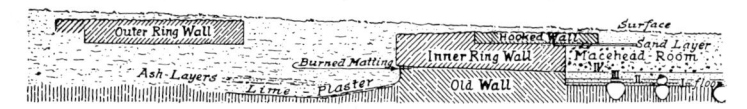

FIG. 23.—Section through inclosure walls and macehead room. Scale, 1:150

construction so far discovered (in i C/9 IV) has not been followed up. On top of it the inner inclosure wall was built. The latter must long have served as the only inclosure of the oval, for the outer wall was not built until the level of the soil outside had become higher. To the next later period belongs a wall built on the ruins of the northeast section of the inner wall. The new wall, however, runs straighter than the old and extends eastward to the outer wall, which must therefore still have existed at that time. At that point the straight wall makes a hairpin turn which is still unexplained. For the present we call this the "hooked wall."

THE OLDER STRUCTURE BENEATH THE INNER WALL

Only along the northeast side of the oval do we have certain knowledge of the existence of the older structure already referred to. There, underneath the inner inclosure wall, we found a wall 3.40 meters wide. Its outer face was followed for about 25 meters and was found to stand .10–.15 behind the outer face of the inner inclosure wall. It could not have served as a foundation for the latter, because at one spot there was an intervening refuse layer (.14 thick) containing sherds and charred remains of matting. It belonged perhaps to an older inclosure wall the ruins of which had been leveled and which had then been renewed on roughly the same scale. Its mode of building cannot be ascertained without destroying important later remains. On the outside the surviving height of the wall is only about .35; it is covered here with a white lime plaster, .002–.003 thick, which is characteristic of this older structure. At the foot of the wall the plaster curves and merges with the coating of a slightly sloping floor about 2 meters wide, underneath which are several easily distinguishable layers of mud plaster. The foot of the wall was thereby well protected against water. Since we observed this arrangement in two spots about 20 meters apart, it probably existed all along the wall.

The inner face common to this older wall and to the inner inclosure wall above it was covered by the hooked wall, which projected .65 over it. In only a few spots could we reach this older structure, which lies about 1 meter below the uppermost layer of the hooked wall. We had occasion to go deeper at one spot because we found there, under a sandy layer .06 thick at the base of the hooked wall, a number of beautiful objects, chiefly maceheads and some important statuette heads (cf. pp. 67–70). We soon realized that we were in the wreckage of a room. Here the inner face of the older wall extends only .16 above the lime floor. It too is coated with white lime plaster, as are the walls of the "macehead room" we had found (see Figs. 22–23). The eastern and western corners of this room (Fig. 24) are still partially masked by later brickwork.

Four successive floor levels, all with remains of lime pavement, show that this room was used for a considerable length of time. In the deepest floor three large pottery storage jars were imbedded to their shoulders. Two were empty, but the third was filled to the brim with burned lime, certainly a very valuable material at that time. Over the mouth of the middle jar stood a rather small pot containing four maceheads; two more maceheads lay on the floor beside it; and many others came out of the overlying rubbish. To this earliest level belonged two short whitewashed mud walls which projected into the room from its northwest wall.[1] The second floor lay at the level of the mouths of the pots. The third level, .07 above the second, survived only at the north corner of the room. The fourth, remains of which

FIG. 24.—The macehead room

could be recognized in the west corner, lay .22 above the pots. To judge from the conditions in the north corner something must have happened that led to a renovation of the building. The inner inclosure wall was then constructed, and the macehead room was restored at the level of the fourth floor. The room remained in use until it finally fell into decay and was leveled when the later hooked wall was constructed.

In the refuse, chiefly in the layer .45 thick between the fourth floor level and the sand on which the hooked wall was built, were found

[1] For the positions of these walls and of the three storage jars see Figs. 22 and 24. The jars are shown in Fig. 23 also.

altogether some forty maceheads, besides statuettes (e.g., Fig. 25), heads (e.g., Figs. 26–27), and a few other objects, which seemed to have been thrown in on purpose. Since underneath the fourth floor level two separate maceheads and a group of six were found, four at least obviously *in situ*, carefully stored in a pot, we must assume that this room served from the beginning as a magazine of valuable products of the stonecutter. Many of the objects lying in the débris above may originally have stood along the walls, perhaps in niches. The fact that the front part of the large head shown in Figure 26 lay 1.70 meters away from the fragments which belonged to it and were

FIG. 25.—Upper part of alabaster figure K. 280. Scale, 3:10

found at the same level, indicates that that head was purposely broken and thrown away. The nature of the building to which the macehead room belongs cannot be determined until more of it has been uncovered.

The head just referred to (K. 279; see Fig. 26) is particularly well modeled and unusually large for its period, being about two-thirds of natural size. The back of the head (missing) was made from a separate piece, attached by a peg; a similar arrangement was used to join the head to the missing body. The eyeballs are cut from shell. The eyelids are of inlaid bitumen, which renders admirably lids covered with the black cosmetic which we know that the Sumerians used, just as the modern Iraqis use *kohl* for the same purpose. We ourselves have

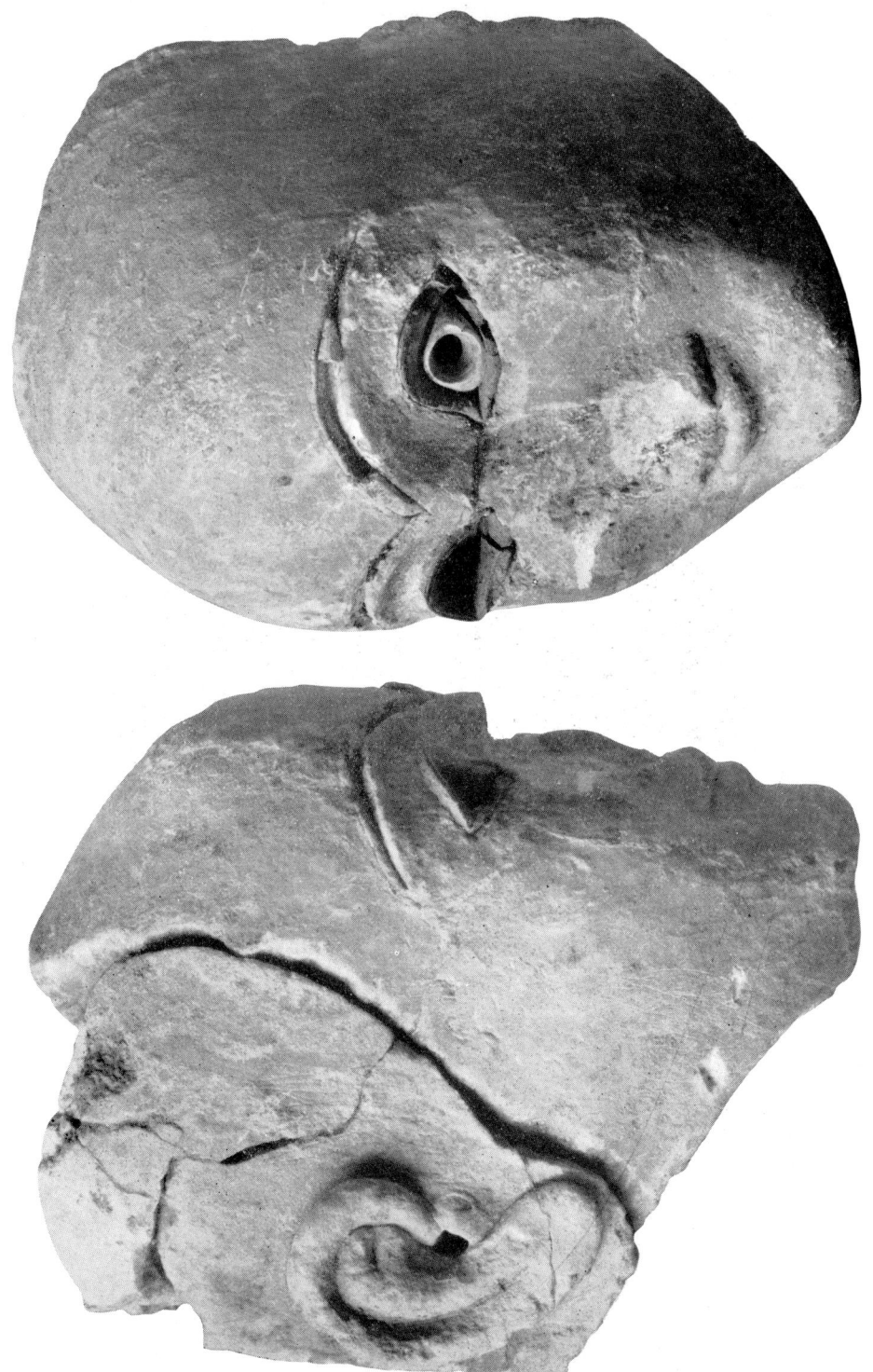

FIG. 26.—Large alabaster head K. 279. Actual size

found alabaster toilet jars containing such cosmetic. Bits of one inlaid lapis lazuli eyebrow remain.

The small head K. 219 (see Fig. 27) is equally sensitively modeled. One pupil of lapis lazuli is still in place. The nature of the yellowish, flaky material used for the eyeballs is not yet determined. The eyelids here are cut in the stone. A similar head showed on the top traces of bitumen which may conceivably have served to attach a separately made wig of other material.[1]

The bust of a bearded figure (K. 280; see Fig. 25), found next to the large head K. 279, shows that long, wavy hair was worn parted

FIG. 27.—Alabaster head K. 219. Actual size

in the middle, hanging in locks in front of the shoulders. It is very similar to pieces (now in Chicago and Baghdad) found by illicit diggers at Khafaje before our work started. Most of the Khafaje statues are made in more than one piece; our bust has a hole in the underside for the peg which was to join it to the skirted lower part.

Contemporary with the building to which the macehead room belonged is an interesting circular water basin of baked brick (Fig. 28) which was discovered at the very beginning of the excavations before the inclosure walls were found. The walls of the basin had been exposed long before our expedition started work and had invited plunderers. As a result of their activities it has not been possible to establish a connection between this basin and the macehead room.

[1] Cf. Mr. Woolley's finds recorded in *op. cit.* X (1930) 324.

South of the basin is a rectangular projection, 2.40×1.80 meters, again built of baked bricks, which, like the bricks of the basin, are laid in bitumen. The inside and the outside of the basin, and also the projection, were coated with bitumen. This baked brick structure had

FIG. 28.—Circular basin in i B/9 IV

probably been purposely destroyed, as bricks laid in bitumen usually survive the most violent weathering. Later it was rebuilt with the floor of the new basin .20 above the old floor. The southern projection as rebuilt was only 1.30×1.60 meters. On the north of the basin we found a drain over a length of 3.50 meters. Parts of it must belong to a later floor level, as they lie .20 higher than the edge of the old basin. Just inside the inner inclosure wall we found, by tunneling, a channel of burned bricks which lies .15 deeper than the northern edge of the basin. Further excavations will no doubt show a connection between the channel and the drain from the basin. One may surmise that the basin and its appendages served some ritual purpose. Among remains of brickwork west of the basin we found in i A/9 IV two courses of a square pedestal oriented like the macehead room.

The filling and leveling of ruined earlier structures which began with the construction of the hooked wall and which we have observed in the layers of the macehead room apparently took place over a somewhat extensive area. Without intending at this time to investigate the earlier period more closely, we did penetrate the rubbish layers near the basin and between it and the inner inclosure wall at spots not covered by later walls and where robbers had already made pits. We found here various objects the presence of which can be explained as in the case of those in the macehead room. Their level corresponded with that of the finds in the macehead room, and among them was a stone macehead.

THE INNER INCLOSURE WALL

The inner inclosure wall was first encountered in i B/9 IV. Its outer face could be followed eastward to the point where it disappeared underneath the hooked wall. Beneath it up to that point lay the older wall. The inner face of the inner inclosure wall has been exposed only in the northern corner of the macehead room; for the rest we confined ourselves to following it to the southwest gateway, avoiding penetrating deeper levels so as not to anticipate the investigation of the interior of the oval, which will be the object of a later campaign.

The wall is built in very careless fashion and apparently without any rules. The mud bricks are laid flat, serving as headers, with scattered instances of stretchers on the wall front. Diagonally laid bricks are not found on the surface, but within the wall occur large or small groups of bricks tilted in various directions and surrounded by layers of bricks laid flat. Especially characteristic of this manner of building are long vertical joints running with the wall, so that it seems to have been built not in horizontal courses but by adding successive vertical "shells" of mud brick till the wall reached its proper thickness.

FIG. 29.—The inclosure walls, looking northwest

This would explain also the distinctive concentric bulges seen in Figure 29. The width of the wall varies considerably as a result of these irregularities (3.40–4.50 meters). This method of building can still be observed in the neighborhood of Basra where the fellahin build dams against rising water, using river mud cut out with their shovels.

The inner inclosure wall could not be traced from i B/9 IV toward the northwest because of later brickwork which we felt should be left for another campaign. As we had found a gateway on the opposite side of the oval, on this side we may expect to find another important

FIG. 30.—Kiln adjoining macehead room

point in the wall, namely, an approach from the town. Where there is a gate there are usually drains. We found here, indeed, only a few centimeters below the surface of the mound a rather late drain of burned brick traversing the wall. It was poorly constructed from unsuitable previously used material: plano-convex burned bricks of varying sizes, among them bricks .32–.335×.17×.05–.08, mingled with curved fragments which seem to have belonged to large earthenware pipes. At lower levels two more drains were found. In the higher strata a solid brick block 1.50 meters wide was built in front of the wall. This widening, taken in conjunction with the drains, can hardly be explained otherwise than by assuming that a gate belonging to the

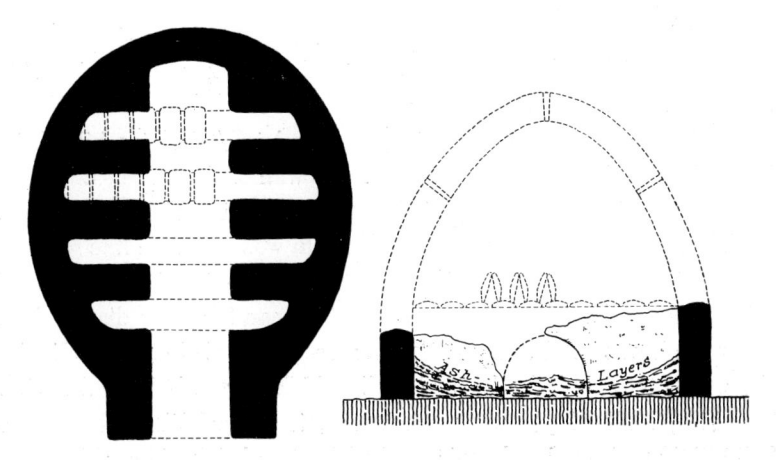

FIG. 31.—Reconstruction of kiln. Scale, 1:50

FIG. 32.—Group of three copper statuettes K 35/a-c

period of the hooked wall existed here. The block consists of four courses of bricks, alternately headers and stretchers, measuring .14–.15×.21–.22×.04–.06.

Farther southeast, between i C/9 IV and i C/9 V, at a kiln (Fig. 30) which partially overlies the southeast wall of the macehead room, three successive building periods are distinguishable. This room, therefore, was already a ruin when the kiln was built. In like manner today kilns are regularly situated outside the inhabited areas of oriental towns, among ruins where rubbish can be easily disposed of. After the kiln ceased to be used, the area was leveled and filled in for the construction of the hooked wall, which covers half of the kiln. The kiln, built of plano-convex bricks, is shaped like a horseshoe 2.70×2.20 meters. Its door is flanked by two brick piers which lean a little toward each other. It was probably spanned by a small arch as suggested in our reconstruction (Fig. 31). Since no sherds or "wasters" were found in the kiln or in its neighborhood, it seems unlikely that pots were baked here. A few fragments of baked bricks found in the ash layers suggest that it served for baking bricks.

Following the inside of the inner inclosure wall we came upon three copper statuettes (Fig. 32) .25 below the surface. They constituted the most imposing find of the campaign. The fact that they had been packed into as small a bundle as possible (Fig. 33) shows clearly that they were highly valued and were hidden away in some emergency such as a hostile invasion. The débris of the mud brick walls above them formed a hard mass of caked mud which preserved them in excellent condition.

The largest statue, now in the museum at Baghdad, is .36 high without its stand, the smaller ones .28 and .29. The latter show men whose hair hangs down to the nape of the neck, whereas the large figure wears a long curly lock hanging down in front of each ear and has the rest of his head shaved. All the figures wear long beards and are naked except for horizontally striped girdles. From the head of the large figure rises what seems to be a four-armed support for a bowl or similar object. The small figures show traces of similar supports. The four-legged stand underneath the large figure is the narrowest of the three. A similar copper support, but five-legged and used for a

FIG. 33.—The three copper statuettes as found. Scale, 1:3

stone vase, was found at Kish underneath the "inundation clay deposit" and is now in the Baghdad Museum.

Professor Cecil H. Desch, F.R.S., professor of metallurgy in the University of Sheffield, who for some years has been engaged in analyses of ancient metals and ores for the Sumer Committee of the British Association for the Advancement of Science, has kindly analyzed the metal of these statues. He finds:

Copper	99%
Tin	00.63%
Lead and iron	traces
Nickel	nil

These figures, then, consist of almost pure copper. Professor Desch says that a slight amount of tin has occasionally, though rarely, been found heretofore in Sumerian copper, that the tin here was certainly not added intentionally, but that the presence of tin in copper ore is unusual. As we learn more about the sources of ore in Western Asia, this unusual compound may help us to find the place where the Sumerians obtained their raw material. Without doubt, the three statuettes were cast in a mold, for on the soles of the feet are small lumps of copper left from the casting. The mold must have been rather complicated. The pedestals, however, were forged of copper, their separate parts welded together. The feet of the figures, in turn, were welded to the pedestals.

The use of the figures can perhaps best be compared with that of pottery stands found in the archaic Ishtar temple at Assur. In both cases offerings may have been placed upon them. Since votive plaques found at Ur, Nippur, Lagash, and elsewhere show naked priests pouring libations before the gods, we may explain the attitude and attire of our figures by assuming that these offering-stands in the form of priests were placed before the cult statue.[1]

On the southwest the inner inclosure wall has a gateway (cf. Fig. 22) the construction of which shows that the builders were well versed in the art of fortification, for this of course was a vital point. Behind the actual gateway was built a large guardroom. Of the door jambs

[1] [The cleaning of the large statue by Herr W. König in the Baghdad Museum has revealed traces of an archaic inscription which has not yet been deciphered.—H. F.]

FIG. 34.—U-shaped drain in guardroom

nothing has been preserved; but a drain which winds through this room, passing presumably through the centers of its two gateways, enables us to fix the positions of the latter. It appears that they were not on the same axis, as was usual later, but were staggered. This made the entrance more easily defensible and also prevented those outside from observing what happened inside the wall. Similar arrangements may still be observed at the entrances to modern houses in the Orient. The fortified gateway within an inclosure wall, which here appears for the first time, is a prototype of the later gateways of Babylonian and Assyrian times, which were perfected by the addition of towers but had their two gateways arranged on a common axis.

The walls of the guardroom are 1.50 meters thick on an average. The short walls continue beyond the inner wall for about 1 meter; near the east corner, the walls show traces of whitewash. The drain (Fig. 34) consists of well laid earthenware troughs .60–.84 long, .17–.24 wide, and .08–.10 high. Baked bricks of various sizes (.15×.22×.03–.06 with two finger marks and .12–.15×.28×.03–.06 with one finger mark), some headers, some stretchers, lie on the edges of the earthenware troughs, practically at the surface of the mound. Probably the drain was originally covered with burned bricks of the larger type; but we know that in the main gateway in the inclosure wall itself the drain was covered by an arch of radially placed plano-convex bricks. The last trough leads into an earthenware pipe .66 long and .205 in diameter, with its farther end reduced to .18 in diameter so that it could be fitted into a similar pipe. The drain is .51 lower at the outer than at the inner gateway. Its slope is thus much steeper than that of an older, lower drain which it meets inside the room and in which it is imbedded for the remainder of its course. This arrangement shows that the level behind the gate was once raised about .30 and that the resulting difference in levels was overcome by providing the room with a sloping floor. This view is supported by the remains of a thin floor surface of very irregularly laid mud bricks preserved in the northwest part of the room and, on the opposite side, by a mud floor, framed by brick fragments and rough field stones, which may have served as a sentry post. The older drain consists of a layer of mud .70 wide, in the middle of which a channel is cut. The whole was then covered with a thick layer of bitumen. A shouldered earthenware pot (.55 high and

.52 in diameter) with upright spout, an unusually large copper vessel (K. 379), and a cylinder seal (K. 386) belonged to the earlier period.

The bitumen drain was picked up again outside the inclosure walls. Here for a distance of 9 meters a vault of plano-convex bricks is still intact, the vault having a breadth of .70 for the first 4 meters, then narrowing to .25 (Fig. 35). Similar drains have been found at Fara.[1]

FIG. 35.—Vaulted brick drain outside southwest gateway

It would seem that this was the main drain of the oval, and it would be important for the topography of the ruins to know its destination and whether it was connected with a larger system of drains. A curious limestone head (K. 536; Fig. 36) was found near here, only .30 below the surface of the mound. No attempt had been made to render details, but otherwise it is very similar to, and therefore probably contemporaneous with, the bust K. 280 (see Fig. 25).

Northwest of the gateway was an open space. The wall which bounded it on the northeast was followed as far as the later drain,

[1] Heinrich and Andrae, *op. cit.* p. 11 and Figs. 8–9.

which crosses it; probably it continued beyond the drain. In this open space two oval structures of plano-convex mud bricks were found; between them stood a squarish pedestal (Fig. 37). The intervening

Fig. 36.—Bearded head K. 536. Scale, 2:5

Fig. 37.—Looking south over open space northwest of southwest gateway

spaces were covered with .10–.20 of fine ashes. Each of the two oval structures had a curious little protuberance in the direction of its main axis. These structures stood .35–.50 above a mud floor which showed traces of whitewash in one spot. Removal of its mud coating showed that the outer wall of the larger structure had been built of two successive vertical "shells" (cf. p. 72). The space within each structure was filled with earth and covered with an uneven mud brick pavement. These brick surfaces had been reddened by large and frequent fires, the ashes from which lay round about. Moreover, the face of the inner inclosure wall near by was hard baked even at floor level, which shows that the fires were not surrounded by protecting walls.

This open space may well have served ritual purposes. The two oval structures may have been used for burnt offerings. The squarish pedestal between would then have been the altar upon which the gifts were consecrated. The only yet known parallels are two structures at Warka.[1] There, however, though the structures belong to the plano-convex brick period, their walls are built of shapeless mud, their floors are of potsherds coated with whitewashed mud, and the pedestal (later in date but supposably replacing an earlier one) stands *inside* the fire area.

Only the beginning of the west curve of the inner inclosure wall could be discerned. The wall seems to have been destroyed at that point by later buildings. Here a baked brick drain with an intake at the east end crosses the wall. Into that drain, but without visible connection, a toilet shaft of large clay rings later penetrated. Beside it lay an interesting round pedestal 1.40 meters in diameter.

THE OUTER INCLOSURE WALL

This wall was constructed after the ground outside the inner inclosure wall had been heightened some .70–.80 by wind-blown sand or accumulated débris (cf. Fig. 23). The two inclosure walls must have existed together for some time. However, by the time the still later hooked wall was built, the inner inclosure wall must already have been in ruins or torn down, while the outer wall still stood undamaged.

The outer inclosure wall exhibits a great advance in the technique of fortification, for the use of towers made possible a far more effective defense than did the smooth face of the inner inclosure wall. But the masonry of the outer wall was no better than that of the older

---

[1] Jordan, *Zweiter vorläufiger Bericht über* .... *Uruk* (Berlin, 1931) pp. 18–19.

structure. There was no foundation; the ground was merely leveled. On the northeast and east, where four courses are preserved, one can see that the bricks were laid flat only. At some points we found a course of headers over a course of stretchers. But often in the midst of regular courses the bricks were laid in utter confusion (cf. e.g., Tower 7, in the foreground of Fig. 38, where one can recognize only a fairly orderly border of headers). The towers do not always start at the same level as the wall. No. 7, for instance, starts two courses

FIG. 38.—Hooked wall and outer inclosure wall, with Tower 7 in foreground

higher. The height of the extant remains of this wall decreases with the slope of the mound as we follow the wall southward and then westward. After Tower 16 there is only one course of bricks; beyond Tower 21 the front of the wall is entirely destroyed. In one spot along the inside of the wall the brickwork descends deeper. There an outer gateway corresponding to the inner one described on pages 78–80 was situated. The drainage which flowed through this southwest gateway had destroyed the door jambs of the outer gateway, where the drain bed has almost disappeared. A parallel for this wall with its planoconvex brick towers has been found at Nippur.[1]

[1] Clarence S. Fisher, *op. cit.* Pl. 4.

One minute bit of evidence has enabled us to make an important observation as to the construction of this wall. On the northeast, where the later houses of the town approach the outer inclosure wall, there was left between the last house and this wall an alley about 2.50 meters wide. In this alley was built a room more than 4 meters long which was probably accessible from the house next to it (cf. Fig. 22). This room fills most of the space between Towers 3 and 4 and includes half of Tower 4. Its floor, covered with bitumen, slopes

Fig. 39.—Outer inclosure wall between Towers 3 and 4, showing niche (behind measuring-rod).

toward the center, where it forms a shallow trough which narrows toward the southeast and ends in an outlet through the cross-wall. The bitumen, .03–.04 thick, covers the bases of the surrounding walls to a height of .15 to protect them from the run-off of the rainfall, which was evidently abundant. This bitumen border, which survived just at the surface of the mound, penetrates at one point into the outer inclosure wall in the form of a doubly recessed niche which lies midway between the two towers (Fig. 39).

This recess is evidently a decorative element such as has been observed in very early Sumerian monumental architecture at Warka[1] and as was used throughout Babylonian and Sumerian times. Only the bitumen coating has preserved this niche, for the brickwork behind it is not preserved so high up. The niche is .40 wide; the depth of the first rebate is .13, of the second, .12. The top of the bitumen is rounded just as it was when the thick mass was smeared on and pressed into place. There is no broken edge which might lead to the conclusion that the whole height of the niche was thus lined, so as to carry off water from the crown of the wall to the trough below. The niche has nothing to do with the basin. It was merely a mural decoration which should be restored above the fifth course in the middle of each curtain wall.

Northwest of Tower 1 the outer inclosure wall breaks off suddenly. Whether this is due to destruction of the gateway which we have assumed at this spot is uncertain. In any case, after an interval of 2.50 meters a mud brick wall begins which is only 1 meter broad and has no towers. It goes somewhat deeper, to be sure, than does the inclosure wall. It does not follow the curve of the inner inclosure wall but runs straight northwest around House D (Fig. 40), then turns straight southwest. We had to stop work just as we again encountered a piece of wall 3.20 meters broad, perhaps the continuation of the outer inclosure wall.

At one point in the narrow wall, a little to one side of the gateway through the inner inclosure wall, a short piece of an old drain bed of bitumen was found. A few meters beyond this we had to leave part of the outer wall unexcavated for the present. Its further course toward the west shows surprising irregularities in thickness around House D. At present we can say only that the wall is not uniform in its construction. It is built partly of slanting bricks alternating with courses of bricks laid flat, like the hooked wall and the interior walls of House D, and partly of bricks laid flat only.

THE HOOKED WALL

This wall was built in a period which had broken with the traditions of the past; a period of decay must have preceded it. The inner inclosure wall with its old buildings then lay in ruins and only the outer

---

[1] Jordan, *op. cit.* p. 48.

FIG. 40.—House D

wall with its towers protected the oval. A new building level, corresponding to the sandy layer over the macehead room, was created by leveling the ruins, in which process all objects sacred to those who had gone before were purposely thrown into the filling. This shows that the later generation wanted to have nothing to do with them or, more probably, that these objects were deposited underneath the new buildings for a magical purpose.

The hooked wall lies partly on the inner inclosure wall and partly inside the oval (cf. Fig. 23). In contrast with the earlier wall, it is built absolutely straight. Both walls are now worn down to the same level, so that the face of the hooked wall, where it was fitted into the inner inclosure wall, could be recognized only after careful clearing of the uppermost layer of mud bricks. It is quite plain that in preparing for the foundations of the hooked wall the brickwork of the older wall was removed only in so far as was absolutely necessary.[1]

The hooked wall, 2.50 meters wide, is distinguished by the great regularity of its courses. The size and shape of the plano-convex bricks remain unchanged. A certain degree of bonding was attained by beginning with a course of headers followed by a course of stretchers and another of headers. The avoidance of continuous joints was left more or less to chance. Above these came three courses of bricks set diagonally in herringbone pattern. Flat courses apparently followed, only one of which is preserved, and that at the highest point.

Beyond the drains which we described in our discussion of the inner inclosure wall (p. 74), the hooked wall continues to the south corner of House D in h E/9 IV. That this section belongs to the hooked wall is shown by its thickness (2.50–2.60 meters) and its mode of construction. Here, however, two courses of flat bricks alternate with two courses of slanting ones. Moreover, definite towers occur, one of which is preserved in Room II and another in Room X of House D. No trace of the inner inclosure wall was found here; both it and the outer inclosure wall in this section seem to have been entirely destroyed. A few irregular fragments of brickwork belonging to the level of the hooked wall were found above the macehead room.

[1] In some places one imagines that one can discern projecting towers, but they are too irregular in shape to permit certainty.

HOUSE D

House D (cf. Figs. 22 and 40) had to be excavated in the short period between February 1 and March 3. Considering the extraordinary richness of our finds, this period was not sufficient for a complete investigation. We determined the situation and plan of the house and made significant observations and finds such as rarely occur in such quantity compressed into so small a space, but our investigation of the outer wall on the northwest and northeast and its relation to the abutting house walls was not completed. The house was built against the hooked wall without regard to its curtains and towers, though it is obvious that the meeting of walls at acute angles was avoided as much as possible. This explains the position of the southeast wall of Room II. Again the irregularities in the thickness of the outer wall are not in keeping with the uniform construction of the house. It would appear, therefore, that the house was built later than either the northern portion of the hooked wall or the present outer wall in a space which may have been left open for such a purpose. The house is obviously important because of its preferred location in the immediate neighborhood of the oval, the strong fortifications of which prove that it contained structures of great significance. As analogies from other Sumerian ruins are still lacking and as a final account of the house as a whole cannot yet be given, we limit ourselves to presenting such observations as we have made.

The entrance to the house was probably at the east, where the hooked wall and the outer wall of the oval begin to diverge. From there the dignitary whom we imagine to have been its occupant would have had easy access to the oval through its northeast gateway. Though later brickwork, including two bitumen-coated water basins (B 1 and B 2 in Fig. 22), covers the older walls here, it seems possible to distinguish a corridor leading into the house. The main rooms are grouped round a central court (Room VIII) the corners of which are oriented to the points of the compass. A great conflagration evidently compelled the inhabitants to evacuate the house so hurriedly that they had to leave all their possessions. They themselves seem to have perished thereby, perhaps at the hand of an enemy. Otherwise they would certainly have tried to rescue their more valuable possessions, such as beads and other ornaments, after the fire, or they would have rebuilt the house. As it is, this did not happen until after débris and wind-blown sand had piled up in the court. Of the reconstruction very little remains, as it lies even with the present surface of the mound. The original house is comparatively well preserved, especially those rooms (Rooms II, VI, VII, IX, and XI) the mud walls of which were baked by the fire.

ROOMS I AND III

On top of Room I (the entrance?) and the neighboring Room III stands a later kiln similar to, but smaller than, the one found over the macehead room. Here some of the plaster of the vaulting over the baking-chamber, almost vitrified, is preserved. Since it would seem that the heating gases were drawn off through a wide opening, we may perhaps assume here a closed fire instead of a grate. The kiln was filled with a whitish gray, granular substance which was chemically analyzed by Dr. Koch, of the chemical laboratory of the State Museums in Berlin, as follows:

	PER CENT
Inorganic residue, mainly sand	21.05
Iron oxide (Fe_2O_3) plus a small amount of aluminium oxide (Al_2O_3)	5.82
Calcium oxide (CaO)	29.25
Magnesium oxide (MgO)	4.59
Phosphoric acid (P_2O_5)	1.58
Sulphuric acid (SO_3)	1.93
Lost in heating (including 23.41 per cent carbon dioxide [CO_2])	32.68
Potassium (K), Sodium (Na), Chlorine (Cl), determined by difference	3.10
	100.00

It appears, then, that the chief constituent was calcium carbonate. This would mean that the kiln was used to burn lime for plaster. We have seen that lime plaster was already in use in the period of the macehead room.

ROOM II

This room, opening from our supposed entrance passage, was perhaps used by servants or guards. Walls and floor are covered with mud plaster. A small, narrow mud wall projects into the room from the hooked wall. Against the northwest wall there is a small mud hearth on which food was prepared. A heap of blue-black mussel shells might be the remains of a meal. Next to the hearth were found in a potsherd charred remains of seeds (K. 450). Professor E. Schiemann of the Botanical Museum in Berlin very kindly investigated our botanical finds in detail and compared them with freshly charred seeds of similar nature. She found that these seeds were derived from a crucifer, *Brassica* or *Sinapis*. Oil pressed from these seeds may have been used in preparing food and for fuel in lamps. Near the hearth were found also some small basalt hand mills, stone and clay pots, bone utensils, and a large shell which had been wrought into a lamp. A round hole .05 in diameter in the bottom of the lamp is filled by a piece of lead with projections which may have fixed it to a foot of clay or bitumen.

The eastern corner of the room was cut off, perhaps for storage purposes, by a thin wall .55 high, rounded at the top. Near by lay a copper fishhook and a large basalt hand mill with its rubber. Not far from the door was found the bottom of a large pot at least .60 in diameter which probably held the water used in this primitive kitchen. In the débris caused by the fire lay several bits of mud ceiling-plaster, now baked, bearing reed impressions. With them were numerous wasps' nests, likewise baked and bearing impressions of matting. Such finds, unimpressive as they are, give us important information as to the ceiling construction, as we shall see presently when discussing Room VII (p. 94).

ROOM VI

The floor of Room VI is .27 below that of Room I. In the western corner were found the remains of a large cylindrical pot. Among the nondescript sherds lying on the floor there appeared a small group of objects which had probably been stored in a pot. Included were a cylinder seal (K. 514) and a copper pin (K. 503) for which parallels are found at Fara and in Cemetery A at Kish. In the eastern corner of the room we succeeded in disentangling the remains of a fishing net. On beginning the excavations we had found in our trial trench in k B/9 IV (cf. Fig. 19) at a depth of 1–1.30 meters numerous clay rings about .065 in diameter, with a circular cross-section about .02 in diameter. Another type was a little smaller (diameter about .052).

Such rings now appeared in House D in great quantities, but not along the inclosure walls. On the floor of Room VI we found, on and beside a large stone about 1 meter below the surface, roughly fifty rings close together. One could observe upon looking carefully that there were some semblances of order (Fig. 41, foreground). It became evident also that in between the rings charred threads remained. A careful investigation on a day when there was no wind brought to light two

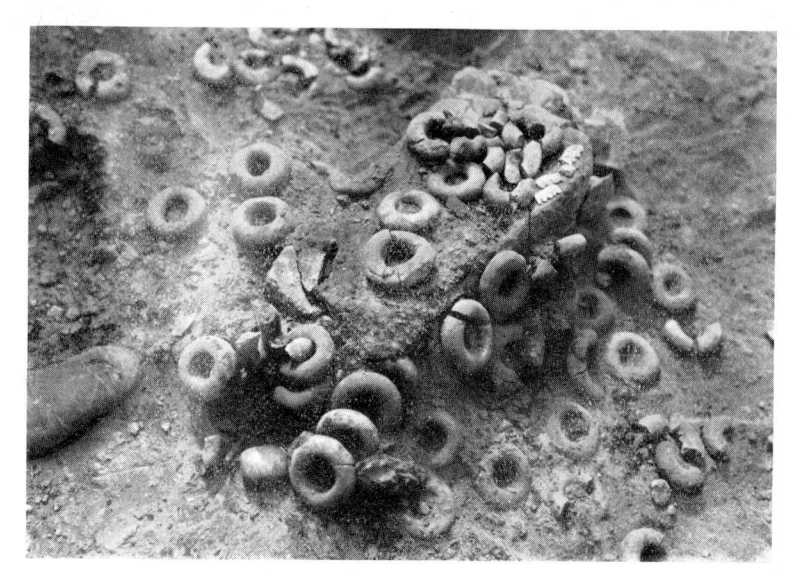

FIG. 41.—Baked clay net-sinkers as found

rings, better protected than the rest, to which threads were still clinging (Fig. 42). Since in one instance the threads clearly form a knot, it is certain that the rings were tied to the net as sinkers. The thread cannot, of course, be compared to the fine hemp thread used by modern fishermen. It is a coarse twine, about .005 thick, which was pulled double through the ring and then knotted. Further study of remains which we have preserved may show at what intervals the rings were fastened to the net.

Our last doubt as to the identity of the fishing net was removed when we discovered, behind the stone upon which it lay, a piece of charred wood (K. 645), now .20×.10×.055, but certainly larger before the fire, with a clean-cut oval hole (.04×.045) in its flat surface. It can have served only as a float to keep the upper edge of the net at the surface of the water. Several such floats would, of course, be needed for a net. The survival of this single one is doubtless due to the fact that it lay deeper than the rest, away from the air, so that it was only partially burned, that is, charred. Thus by great good fortune

Fig. 42.—Sinkers with twine attached

the conflagration preserved for us remains which, had they not been charred, would long ago have perished.

ROOM VII

We ascend a step of .16 to reach Room VII. Like all the rooms in this house, none of its corners is rectangular. The bricks here were .15×.22; we could not be certain of their height. The southeast wall, at least, was built without foundation; the plaster begins above the lowest two courses of bricks, and only after the completion of the plastering was the floor filled in, rising .32 above the lowest course. In the middle of the northwest part of the room lay four large basalt hand mills measuring about .72×.35×.12. Their rubbing surfaces had been worn smooth by long use; their undersides had been rounded off but left rough. All four had been shattered by the heat of the fire. Two more, each with its rubber, lay by the southeast wall of Room IX, and a seventh in Room X. They are grain mills and seem rather too numerous for one household. Perhaps a large community had to be provided with flour from here. Charred remains of grain were found in the western corner of Room XI, in the northwest part of Room IX, and in the southwest part of Room VII. Here they were spread out on a reed mat which was likewise charred.

In some spots parts of the fallen ceiling could be recognized among the débris. A continuous piece found east of the door leading into Room VIII shows the remains of two charred ceiling-beams which had rested on the two long walls and had scarcely changed their relative positions when they fell. They seem to have been at least .20 thick, and the interval between them is no more than that. Across the beams, that is, in the direction of the long axis of the room, and at a height of about .20, a thick layer of reeds, still preserved in charred condition to a thickness of .02 in places, was spread over layers of clay. In the débris we found also wasps' nests and some peculiarly shaped clay fragments, few of them more than .10–.15 long, which had been baked by the fire. In cross-section these fragments show a concave base surmounted by a flattened ellipse. The concave surfaces bear unmistakable impressions of the ceiling-beams, which were evidently tree trunks. Stripped trunks of poplars from the mountains of Kurdistan are even today much in demand for ceiling-beams. One of these bits of clay finally gave us the surprising solution to its curious curves. It was still attached to a charred piece of reed matting .07 long and to a wasp's nest which bore upon its surface a sharp impression of the continuation of the reed mat (Fig. 43). Now wasps like to build their nests in angles and corners at the highest points in a room. It is clear, then, that the pieces of clay were stuck to the beams to broaden the bearings of the overlying reed mat so as to prevent its sagging and tearing. One wonders whether these clay attachments could stand vertical pressure from above without a fastening of some sort. In our reconstruction (see Fig. 43) we have assumed that wooden dowels were used to fasten them to the beams, though none have been found yet. Both this patch of ceiling, protected for the summer by corrugated iron, and the unexplored adjoining area may provide further details.

ROOM IX

The southwest doorway of Room VII leads into Room IX, the largest room of the house. Part of its pavement, of small pebbles covered with bitumen, was found in front of the doorway to Room XI. Near the southern corner the wall shows a white lime plaster, preserved for only a few centimeters above the floor and overlapping the adjoining door jambs.

Near the southeast wall of this room we found the two basalt hand mills mentioned on page 93. Four meters west of them lay the fine

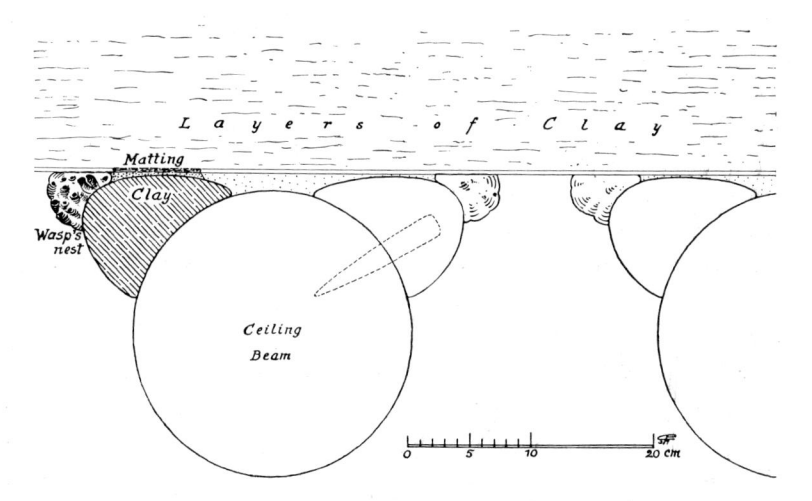

FIG. 43.—Reconstruction of ceiling detail in House D. Scale, 1:6

alabaster relief K. 400 (Fig. 44). Similar rectangular votive tablets have been found at Nippur,[1] Tello,[1] and Ur.[2] They were attached horizontally to a floor or platform, or vertically to a wall, by a peg passing through the central hole. Our tablet shows on back and sides traces of bitumen, which evidently served as an additional means of fastening it in place. This relief had been kept in the room after it was broken and one corner had been lost; for the fragments as found lay in two groups (one upside down) the originally contiguous edges of

[1] H. Schäfer and W. Andrae, *Die Kunst des alten Orients* (Berlin, 1925) pp. 454–55.

[2] Woolley, *op. cit.* VI (1926) Pl. LIII.

96   Khafaje

which were damaged, whereas the edges of the more recent breaks within the groups, due simply to the weight of later débris above them, were sharp. The course of the old crack through opposite corners of

Fig. 44.—Alabaster votive tablet K. 400. Scale, 2:5

the central hole shows that the tablet had been broken by the use of too large a peg.

This exceedingly interesting tablet, now in the Baghdad Museum, can be completely reconstructed by means of the corresponding corner of a fragment (Fig. 45) found by Mr. Woolley at Ur and now in the museum of the University of Pennsylvania at Philadelphia.[1]

The upper register of our tablet shows a banquet in progress. The seated figure on our right is no doubt the king. His hair is dressed like that in Figure 25, or perhaps he wears a wig. The shape of his cup reminds one of the silver cups from the royal tombs at Ur. In his left hand he holds a bunch of dates. The seated figure opposite him is no doubt his queen; she wears her hair in a style similar to that of head K. 562 in Figure 49. The other figures are two butlers, a harper, and the queen's attendant.

Fig. 45.—Fragment of limestone votive tablet found by Woolley at Ur and now in the museum of the University of Pennsylvania.

In the middle register we see at our left two men carrying a heavily laden vessel suspended from a pole which bends under its weight.[2] At our right a goat is followed by a man carrying a load (probably a pot) on his head and a dagger in his right hand. In the background grows a plant bearing a bud and a seven-petaled flower such as appears in more or less conventionalized form on the diadem,[3] the gaming-board,[4] the "standard,"[5] and other objects from Ur. Comparison of these

[1] *Antiquaries Journal*, Vol. VIII (1928) Pl. V and Vol. IX (1929) Pl. II.

[2] Cf. a cylinder seal in Heinrich and Andrae, *op. cit.* Pl. 64.

[3] *Museum Journal* XIX (1928) 380.

[4] *Antiquaries Journal* VIII (1928) Pl. LV.   [5] *Ibid.* Pl. LIX.

scenes with those on the "standard" from Ur suggests that this register shows how food and drink were brought to the royal banquet. But it may be ritualistic instead, representing the bringing of libations and of the sacrificial animal. A votive tablet from Nippur[1] shows a very similar animal scene.

The lowest register is astonishingly like the fragment from Ur (see Fig. 45). Now that our relief supplies the heads, the nature of the animals in the Ur fragment becomes less disputable. Mr. Woolley called them lions,[2] and Mr. Gadd spoke of asses.[3] Though the head shapes and the short ears suggest horses, the tails are more like those of asses. Our choice is evidently limited to horses, asses, or mules.

A badly damaged alabaster head (K. 399) offered further proof that in Room IX were stored objects which had seen their best days. Pottery vessels contained groups of objects. K. 454, for example, held some small, beautifully shaped jars of white limestone, black stone, or pottery, together with worn sea-snail shells, which had served as bowls, and other shells and beads. In the west corner there was a heap of sea-snail shells which may have served as raw material for a shell-cutter. In the northwest part of the room remains of charred seeds were found. Professor Schiemann identified them as *Linum usitatissimum* (flax). They are distinguished from similar seeds by the location and structure of the embryo. They are not flat like fresh linseed; the charring had caused them to swell almost to a pear shape because of their oil content, but it was found that the charring of fresh linseed produces the same effect. The finding of these seeds suggests that flax was already used for textiles, while the linseed was used for oil. Charred remains of reed mats from the ceiling were found here also.

Between the northeast corner and the doorway leading into the court an almost semicircular buttress projects into the room. We do not yet know whether it consists of mud brick like the very similar find in Court 6 of the Sumerian palace in Mound A at Kish, but it certainly belongs to the original plan of the house. Remains of a later period included a piece of bitumen floor coating, 4×1.30 meters, between the two doorways of the southwest wall .46 over the old floor

---

[1] Schäfer and Andrae, *op. cit.* p. 454.

[2] *Antiquaries Journal* VIII (1928) 18.

[3] *History and Monuments of Ur* (London, 1929) p. 31.

level and above the débris of the fire. In connection with this, traces of bitumen visible within the core of the wall for a distance of 1.60 meters suggest that perhaps Room X, which was not burned and must therefore have been habitable after the fire, was now made accessible through the wall because its original doorway was choked with débris.

ROOM X

Finds in this room included a basalt hand mill with its rubber and a disk of baked clay .65 in diameter, .05 thick in the middle and .045 thick at its rounded edge, lying on a layer of reddish clay .045 thick. We would consider the disk a potter's wheel if any arrangement for rotating it had been in evidence.

K. 66   K. 559   K. 90

FIG. 46.—So-called "goddess" handles from large pottery jars

ROOM XI

In the middle of this room a large field stone had been let into the floor, perhaps to serve as a worktable. All four corners of the room were filled with objects of daily use, especially pots. Fragments of one large pottery jar show the projecting shoulder, incised ornamentation, and upright free-standing handle (cf. Fig. 46) typical of the "goddess" vases found at Kish.[1] There were also some charred remains of lentils (probably *Lens esculenta*) lying among the fragments of a pottery jar, and of barley (*Hordeum vulgare*)[2] mingled with some spun and woven vegetable fibers, perhaps the remains of a sack in which it had been

[1] Field Museum of Natural History, "Anthropology Memoirs" I 21–24 and Pls. I 5, IX, X.

[2] Our thanks are again due to Professor Schiemann for these identifications.

kept. We found also a clay spindle whorl with pricked-in decoration and six flint saws set in bitumen.

ROOM XII

Of this room we know very little. It seems not to have had any entrance.[1]

ROOM XIII

This room had a hearth against its northeast wall, in front of which there were thick layers of ashes. There are two doorways, one leading into the court, the other into a corridor and thence to an opening in the outer wall through which passed a drain providing for the disposal of waste water from the house. In this room a cylinder seal (K. 476) was found.

ROOM XVI

This room had been enlarged by knocking off some of the "shells" of mud bricks from the outer wall. Its only doorway, the jambs of which are not parallel, was cut through the previously standing outer inclosure wall. Within the room an alcove wall was later built upon accumulated rubbish. In this room were found a copper nail; various shells, one wrought into a bowl; a statuette head of feldspar; two pottery bowls; and half of a polished limestone bowl, coated inside with bitumen, which had been repaired with three lead pot-menders. Such careful repairs show that stone vessels of this sort must have possessed considerable value.

ROOM VIII

This is the open court which formed the center of the house. Though approximately square, none of its corners forms a right angle. Two things strike the eye at once: a pedestal 2 meters in front of the southwest wall and a semicircular platform between the doorways of Rooms XVII and XVIII. The pedestal is not quite centered in the court, but it lies—certainly not by accident—exactly in the axis of the doorway of Room XVIII. The top of the pedestal is weathered away down to the present surface of the mound, so that only .65 of its original height remains. The mud plaster on three of its sides is coated with lime, which extends over the floor around it also to a certain extent. Its fourth side—the northeast—is broken away, hence the

[1] See in Heinrich and Andrae, *op. cit.* p. 13 and Pl. 6, a room the walls of which were preserved to a height of 1.60 meters but showed no doorway.

present oblong outline. Originally this pedestal was probably square like those in i A/9 IV (p. 72) and h E/9 V (p. 82).

The semicircular platform, of baked plano-convex bricks varying in size, rises .20 above the floor level of the court. The bricks form a slightly elevated rim around the platform; the wall is protected against water by a step .20 wide and .08–.10 high. The whole was covered with bitumen, as were parts at least of the court also, to judge by several rather large fragments found there. An outlet in the western rim of the platform leads to a bitumen-lined channel which runs toward the pedestal, but after 3 meters becomes so shallow that it cannot be followed farther. The bottom of a large pottery jar was found on the north part of the platform. Beside it lay three deep pottery bowls, probably ladles. On the other side an impression of basketwork showed where a heavy basket must have stood on the bitumen on a hot summer day. Whatever purpose the platform served, it would seem that water was freely used there.

At the doorway to Room VII we found a large jar (K. 642) similar to, but more elaborate than, that discovered in the guardroom by the southwest gateway of the inner inclosure wall (p. 80). Leaning against the southeast wall of the court were two small pots filled with very small lapis lazuli, agate, and gold beads, seven unusually large lapis lazuli beads, and ten copper rings. The latter resemble those used in the headdress of Queen Shub-ad.[1] That the inhabitants left these ornaments behind suggests that the house was abandoned hurriedly.

ROOMS XIX, V, AND IV

Rooms XIX and V together lead to Room IV, which was partly destroyed by the later kiln (see p. 90). The floor of Room IV was coated with bitumen. A toilet occupied its north corner; and a drain, presumably for a bath, led through its southwest wall into Room I, which must have been an open court.

ROOM XVIII

This most interesting room is distinguished by its straight walls and almost square corners. Three mud-coated steps lead down into the room (Fig. 47). Near the north corner stood what seems to have been an altar, built of plano-convex mud bricks (Fig. 48; cf. Fig. 47).

[1] See Woolley, *op. cit.* VIII (1928) Pl. LXXI.

Fig. 47.—Room XVIII in House D

Fig. 48.—The altar in Room XVIII of House D

The whole of this structure was coated with a thick white lime plaster. That the altar is so well preserved is due to later brickwork about it. The plaster is worn away in the middle of the flat surface only, where offerings were evidently laid. In front of the altar were found seven statuette heads, ten statuettes (some incomplete), one figure of a ram, four amulets in animal form, three stone vases, one stamp seal and one cylinder seal, a double cosmetic-container in animal form, and four other objects. It is possible that there was a ritual connection between this altar and the pedestal in the court (cf. p. 100).

After the conflagration the room floor had been raised to the level of the court. The altar, no longer in use, had been covered over with plano-convex bricks .15×.20×.03–.05, of the one-finger-mark type, laid in alternating stretcher and header courses and extending to the north corner of the room. The bench thus formed, rising .30 above the new floor level and measuring 1.70×.90, was probably used for secular purposes, perhaps to sleep on. The objects mentioned above were actually found in the upper .30 of the filling just below the new floor level. Twelve of them, among them two heads and six statuettes, had been placed carefully side by side near the east corner.[1]

A few of the heads found in this room are shown in Figure 49. After the original nose of head K. 594 had been broken off, a new one was carefully attached by a dowel. But this too did not last; the long dowel, reaching from the forehead to the upper lip, shows an ancient break. The eyeballs are of shell set in bitumen; the left iris, still preserved, is a shell bead in which was set a pupil of bitumen. In the female heads the elaborately dressed hair deserves notice. In K. 562, for example, the front locks are brought forward in curls around the face, while the rest of the hair is combed back and held in place by a headband. It is then put into a hairnet, turned up at the back, and fastened on the top of the head with hairpins. The same fashion is shown in the top row of the relief K. 400 (see Fig. 44). In K. 597 the hair is parted in the middle; short wavy locks hang down over the ears, and the rest is divided into two braids which are wound around the head. The eyes are pieces of shell roughly stuck on instead of inlaid into the sockets. No doubt they represent careless repairs. It is curious that the ladies are without eyebrows, whereas we know that

[1] One may compare the observations made in the macehead room (p. 68).

FIG. 49.—Five alabaster heads found in Room XVIII of House D. Actual size

Sumerian sculptors rendered them usually with great care. Perhaps they were painted on the completed figures.

The miniature bust K. 595 (Fig. 50), cut from an exceptionally thick piece of shell, is perfectly preserved and is truly astonishing in its lifelike portrayal of an elderly man. It is only .032 high. The lines of the shell structure are cleverly utilized to heighten the relief effect of the chest muscles. The groove above the forehead and the excep-

Fig. 50.—Male bust cut in shell. Actual size   K 595

tional lowness of the head can perhaps be explained by assuming that a piece of some other material was fitted on to represent hair or a wig.

PRIVATE DWELLINGS

A few private houses were discovered when a trial trench was cut across the ridge of Mound A (cf. Fig. 19) at the beginning of our excavations. Their presence here at a level higher than that of the presumably older oval corresponds with observations made at other sites that a residence section might rise as much as 2 meters in the course of a few centuries.[1] Rubbish of all kinds was thrown out of the

[1] O. Reuther, *Die Innenstadt von Babylon (Merkes)* (Leipzig, 1926) pp. 75 and 87.

houses into the streets just as is done today in the Orient. Thus the street levels grew higher. Meantime the houses, built of poor material, would collapse, and the next generation would erect its buildings on their ruins.

In such fashion we can explain the houses on our Mound A.[1] The small rooms lie along a lane about 1.50 meters wide, the surface of which has been gradually raised in the manner above described. The houses here too were built of plano-convex bricks laid both flat and slanting. The walls, .80–.90 thick, are coated with mud plaster often just as good as that in House D. Bitumen was sometimes used on floors and drains. We touched also a deeper layer of house foundations, oriented like those in the higher layer. Our program for the season did not include more than the determination of the nature of these structures.

In following the outer inclosure wall we found outside of Towers 3 and 4 one room of a house which we had to investigate further in order to understand its relation to the inclosure wall. It proved to be oriented like the private dwellings farther east on the summit of the mound. It belongs, therefore, to that group and shows that the residential section of the town extended in course of time to the oval. Originally a distance of 2.50 meters seems to have been left between the oval and the house, probably to allow for traffic. Later, when the bitumen basin was built between Towers 3 and 4 (see p. 85), this lane had apparently become unnecessary. The house has a central court in the middle of which is a mud brick dais 2.60 meters long, 1.20 meters wide, and, at present, .40 high. In the short walls of the court we believe we recognized two opposite niches 1.80 meters wide and .20 deep. The trapezoid room southwest of the court was the best preserved. Its floor was covered with bitumen; in a depression in the middle were found sherds of a large pot, no doubt a water jar. From the west side ran a drain of baked brick which turned outside and disappeared under the bitumen basin. This trapezoid room contained all the essentials of a bathroom. Since we had found other bathrooms in House D and even

[1] [It should be remembered, lest the time interval between the building of the oval and the building of the town on Mound A be overrated, that Mound A rises less than 2 meters above the level of the oval.—H. F.]

in the houses along our trial trench, we can safely say that the bath was an essential element of the Sumerian dwelling-house.

The private houses found on Mound A belong to the latest period of habitation on the mound. They were built long after the outer inclosure wall. At least partial contemporaneity with House D is indicated by the finding of similar types of clay net-sinkers and other objects in both areas.

GRAVES

In the eastern half of our trial trench we found near the surface no houses, but a cemetery. Plano-convex bricks appeared again below the burials. The first 12 meters of the trench contained, over its full width of 5 meters and to a depth of 2 meters, irregularly superimposed layers of ashes and charcoal and reddish layers of burned earth interspersed with thin sedimentary layers of sand and clay. The ashes can be due only to burnt offerings made beside the graves after interment, for such skeletons as we discovered show no traces of cremation comparable to finds at Surghul and el-Hibba and more recently at Warka also. Of the few graves found here and in the vicinity, two were well preserved. It appears from these graves that the dead were buried neither in sarcophagi nor in jars. The two undisturbed graves contained children's skeletons lying on their sides in a contracted position as in Cemetery A at Kish. The burial pits were large enough to contain, in addition, abundant and bulky tomb equipment. Each burial was covered with a reed mat, remains of which have survived, and then with earth.

Grave K. 55 (Fig. 51) in k B/9 V, 1 meter deep, contained the well preserved skeleton of a child about ten years old. It lay on its left side, head to the southwest, looking north. Across the pelvis lay a copper dagger (Fig. 52). Its hilt consisted of two pieces of wood (still partially preserved) riveted to the tang and ornamented with hemispherical copper nailheads of the same type as those of a golden dagger from Ur with which ours must be roughly contemporaneous. At the throat lay an agate bead and two unusually large lapis lazuli beads. A copper adz with a strengthening rib on the back, a twisted copper hairpin, a copper finger ring, a hemispherical copper bowl, and three pottery jars were also found in this grave (see Fig. 52). Besides these

FIG. 51.—Grave K. 55

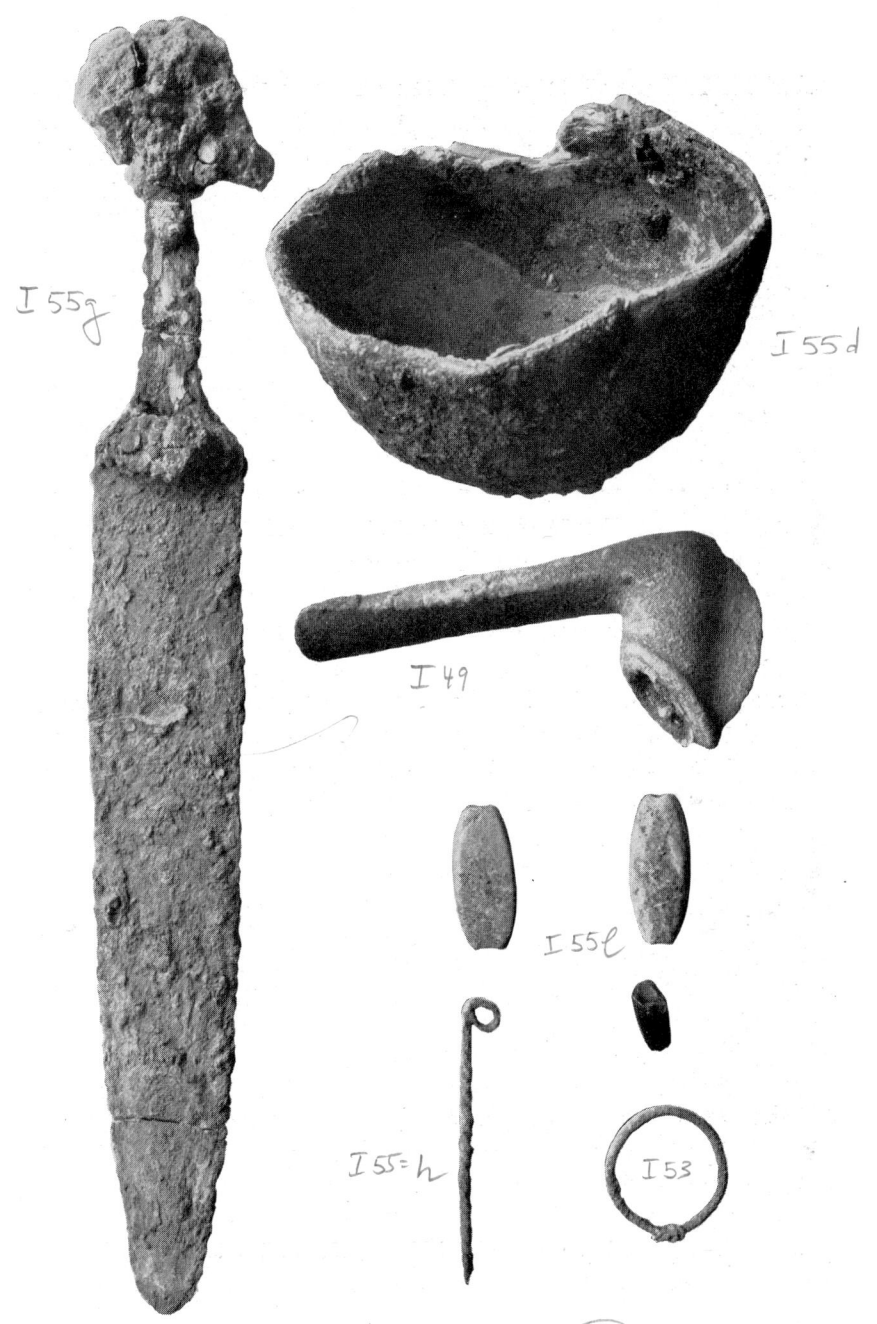

Fig. 52.—Beads and copper objects from Grave K. 55. Scale, 3:5 = Tduo
grave no. 165

110 KHAFAJE

FIG. 53.—Pottery *in situ* in Grave K. 31

FIG. 54.—Inscribed votive macehead K. 636, of hard limestone. Actual size

objects we found on top of the reed mat, that is, outside of the actual burial, two smaller pottery dishes. Remains of burnt offerings were found .22 higher than the skeleton.

The other undisturbed burial (K. 95) was found in k A/9 V beneath plano-convex brickwork, 1.80 meters below the surface of the mound. The well preserved skeleton lay with head to the southeast, looking north. The equipment here consisted of a copper hairpin with head of lapis lazuli (a type common in Cemetery A at Kish), a small handmade conical pot and part of a small clay animal figure (doubtless toys), and eighteen beads of lapis lazuli, agate, and shell.

Objects found in the disturbed graves harmonize with those found in the two just described. Much of the pottery from both the graves and the houses resembles types already known from Cemetery A at Kish.[1] Examples are seen *in situ* in Figure 53.

A beautiful ceremonial macehead of fine white limestone, K. 636 (Fig. 54), was found on one of the last days of the season, only .25 below the surface of the mound. Though we could not connect it with any of the buildings, it is dedicated, as Dr. Jacobsen informs me, to Innanna, the Akkadian Ishtar, which suggests that she was worshiped at Khafaje and that her temple may perhaps be found within the oval.

CONCLUSION

As we review the results of the first campaign at Khafaje, two features appear especially important for the history of Sumer. Firstly, the people of the plano-convex brick period ruled not only the south country from Ur to Kish, but have left evidences of their presence at Khafaje also. The region supposed to have been inhabited by them is thus extended 90 kilometers northward. Secondly, these people contributed no merely transient phase to the history of Mesopotamia. The examples of art found at Khafaje show a mastery which must have required a long time for its development. Our very limited excavations, which went only 1 meter deep, leave no room for doubt that this civilization extended over several centuries. The various periods are best represented by (1) the macehead room with its four floor

---

[1] We found specimens of Mackay's Types A, B, C, E, G, K, L, N, and O. See Field Museum of Natural History, "Anthropology Memoirs" I 21–37 and Pls. IX–XVI.

levels; (2) the inner inclosure wall; (3) the outer inclosure wall with its improved means of defense; (4) the hooked wall; (5) House D; (6) the houses on the summit of Mound A. This succession of periods is clearly recognizable from overlappings of these and intermediate remains upon one another.

In all of our periods plano-convex bricks were used. But it is practically impossible to construct with them such well bonded masonry as is known in Mesopotamia both before and after this epoch. Hence these people presumably used plano-convex brick as a substitute for another building material to which they were accustomed, namely, stones rounded by rushing streams. It follows that these builders must have come into the plain from a mountainous region.

The plano-convex brick period cannot be dated exactly, as the data for events prior to 2300 B.C. are not yet historically comprehensible. The persistent absence of inscriptions from our finds shows that the people of this period took little pleasure in writing. For the time being, then, we are dependent upon comparative material from other Sumerian ruins. We may consider ourselves fortunate that striking parallels for the pottery and the copper objects have been found in Cemetery A at Kish.

We await with the greatest interest further excavations at Khafaje Mound A, which should reveal much concerning the structures within the inclosure walls.

[PRINTED IN U·S·A]

ORIENTAL INSTITUTE SERIES

STUDIES IN ANCIENT ORIENTAL CIVILIZATION
Monographs dealing with various specific phases of the cultures of the ancient Near East

(1) NOTES ON EGYPTIAN MARRIAGE, CHIEFLY IN THE PTOLEMAIC PERIOD. By WILLIAM F. EDGERTON. (Originally called Vol. I, Part I.) x+25 pages, royal 8vo, paper . $1.00

(2) HITTITE HIEROGLYPHS. I. By IGNACE J. GELB. xxii+88 pages, royal 8vo, paper 1.50

(3) DIE HETHITISCHE BILDERSCHRIFT. By EMIL O. FORRER. 62 pages, royal 8vo, paper 1.00

(4) ARCHEOLOGY AND THE SUMERIAN PROBLEM. By HENRI FRANKFORT. 72 pages, royal 8vo, paper 1.00

(5) A NEW INSCRIPTION OF XERXES FROM PERSEPOLIS. By ERNST HERZFELD. viii+14 pages, royal 8vo, paper . . .50

(6) KITĀB AL-ZAHRAH . . . . composed by ABŪ BAKR MUHAMMAD IBN . . . . DĀWŪD. Edited by A. R. NYKL in collaboration with IBRAHĪM ṬŪQĀN. 8+406 pages, royal octavo, paper 2.00

ASSYRIOLOGICAL STUDIES
Philological researches dealing chiefly with cuneiform grammatical and lexicographical material

(1) BEITRÄGE ZUM ASSYRISCHEN WÖRTERBUCH. I. By BRUNO MEISSNER. (Originally called Vol. I, Part I.) 92 pages, royal 8vo, paper $1.00

(2) THE SUMERIAN PREFIX FORMS E- AND I- IN THE TIME OF THE EARLIER PRINCES OF LAGAŠ. By ARNO POEBEL. 47 pages, royal 8vo, paper 1.00

(3) DAS APPOSITIONELL BESTIMMTE PRONOMEN DER 1. PERS. SING. IN DEN WESTSEMITISCHEN INSCHRIFTEN UND IM ALTEN TESTAMENT. By ARNO POEBEL. 86 pages, royal 8vo, paper 1.00

(4) BEITRÄGE ZUM ASSYRISCHEN WÖRTERBUCH. II. By BRUNO MEISSNER. 112 pages, royal 8vo, paper 1.00

ANCIENT RECORDS
English translations of historical documents of the ancient Near East

ANCIENT RECORDS OF EGYPT. Vols. I-V. HISTORICAL DOCUMENTS. By JAMES H. BREASTED. 1,774 pages, royal 8vo, cloth, sold only in sets 22.00

ANCIENT RECORDS OF ASSYRIA AND BABYLONIA. Vols. I and II. HISTORICAL RECORDS OF ASSYRIA. By DANIEL D. LUCKENBILL. 801 pages, royal 8vo, cloth, sold only in sets . . 8.00

Special Library Edition on all-rag paper. Vols. I and II . . . 10.00

ORIENTAL INSTITUTE PUBLICATIONS
Scientific presentations of documents and other source materials

Vol. I. ORIENTAL FORERUNNERS OF BYZANTINE PAINTING. By JAMES HENRY BREASTED. 105 pages, 23 plates, 58 text figures, 4to, boards 4.00

(Continued on cover page four)

THE UNIVERSITY OF CHICAGO PRESS

ORIENTAL INSTITUTE SERIES

ORIENTAL INSTITUTE PUBLICATIONS (*Continued*)

Vol. II. THE ANNALS OF SENNACHERIB. By DANIEL DAVID LUCKENBILL. 196 pages, 4to, boards . . . . $ 4.00

Vols. III and IV. THE EDWIN SMITH SURGICAL PAPYRUS. Edited by JAMES HENRY BREASTED. Two volumes, 4to and folio, cloth 20.00

Vol. V. RESEARCHES IN ANATOLIA. I. EXPLORATIONS IN CENTRAL ANATOLIA, SEASON OF 1926. By H. H. VON DER OSTEN. 167 pages, 24 plates, 242 text figures, 4to, cloth . . . 4.00

Vol. VI. RESEARCHES IN ANATOLIA. II. THE ALISHAR HÜYÜK, SEASON OF 1927. Part I. By H. H. VON DER OSTEN and ERICH F. SCHMIDT. 284 pages, 5 colored plates, 22 maps, 251 text figures, 4to, cloth 8.00

Vol. VII. RESEARCHES IN ANATOLIA. III. THE ALISHAR HÜYÜK, SEASON OF 1927. Part II. By H. H. VON DER OSTEN and ERICH F. SCHMIDT. 134 pages, 1 colored plate, 106 text figures, 4to, cloth 5.00

Vol. VIII. MEDINET HABU. I. EARLIER HISTORICAL RECORDS OF RAMSES III. By the EPIGRAPHIC SURVEY, HAROLD H. NELSON, Field Director. xviii+10 pages, 54 plates, 2 text figures, large folio, cloth 20.00

Vol. IX. MEDINET HABU. II. LATER HISTORICAL RECORDS OF RAMSES III. By the EPIGRAPHIC SURVEY, HAROLD H. NELSON, Field Director. 76 plates, 6 text figures, large folio, cloth 30.00

Vol. X. PREHISTORIC SURVEY OF EGYPT AND WESTERN ASIA. I. PALEOLITHIC MAN AND THE NILE-FAIYUM DIVIDE; A STUDY OF THE REGION DURING PLIOCENE AND PLEISTOCENE TIMES. By K. S. SANDFORD and W. J. ARKELL. 77 pages, 11 plates, 1 map, 4to, cloth 5.00

Vol. XI. CUNEIFORM SERIES. I. SUMERIAN LEXICAL TEXTS FROM THE TEMPLE SCHOOL OF NIPPUR. By EDWARD CHIERA. 126 plates with 256 texts in facsimile, 4to, cloth 5.00

Vol. XII. THE PROVERBS OF SOLOMON IN SAHIDIC COPTIC ACCORDING TO THE CHICAGO MANUSCRIPT. Edited by WILLIAM H. WORRELL. xxx+107 pages, 1 plate, 4to, cloth . 5.00

Vol. XIII. BARHEBRAEUS' SCHOLIA ON THE OLD TESTAMENT. I. GENESIS–II SAMUEL. By MARTIN SPRENGLING and WILLIAM CREIGHTON GRAHAM. xvi+393 pages, 4to, cloth . . 10.00

Vol. XIV. CUNEIFORM SERIES. II. INSCRIPTIONS FROM ADAB. By DANIEL DAVID LUCKENBILL. 87 plates with 198 texts in facsimile, 4to, cloth 5.00

Vols. XV–XVIII in preparation.

Vol. XIX. RESEARCHES IN ANATOLIA. IV. THE ALISHAR HÜYÜK, SEASONS OF 1928 AND 1929. Part I. By ERICH F. SCHMIDT. xxii+294 pages, 47 plates (7 in colors), 377 text figures, 4to, cloth 12.00

THE UNIVERSITY OF CHICAGO PRESS